SCIENCE OF MONEY

Dr. Maxwell Shimba

Published in Manhattan, New York by Shimba Publishing, LLC.

Shimba Publishing, LLC

Printed in the United States of America

First Printing Edition 2024

TABLE OF CONTENTS

INTRODUCTION

UNDERSTANDING THE ESSENCE OF MONEY

Money is more than just a medium of exchange; it is a cornerstone of economic systems, a driver of human behavior, and a critical component of financial stability and growth. The science of money delves into its origins, functions, and the intricate systems that govern its use. This chapter provides an overview of the fundamental concepts and historical developments that have shaped our understanding of money, setting the stage for a deeper exploration of its role in the modern economy.

The Evolution of Money

From Barter to Currency

In the earliest economies, barter was the primary method of exchange. People traded goods and services directly, but this system had significant limitations.

- Double Coincidence of Wants: Barter requires that each party has something the other wants.

- Indivisibility of Goods: Some items cannot be easily divided to facilitate trade.

- Lack of Standardization: Determining the relative value of diverse goods was challenging.

To overcome these limitations, societies developed commodity money—items with intrinsic value that could be universally accepted. Examples include:

- Shells and Beads: Used by various cultures as a medium of exchange.

- Precious Metals: Gold and silver coins became standardized forms of money due to their durability, divisibility, and intrinsic value.

The Advent of Coinage and Paper Money

The introduction of coinage around 600 BCE marked a significant advancement. Coins were stamped with images to verify their authenticity and value, facilitating easier and more reliable trade.

- Uniformity: Coins had a standardized weight and purity.

- Portability: Easier to carry compared to bulky barter items.

- Durability: Precious metals are resistant to wear and degradation.

The development of paper money in China during the Tang Dynasty (618–907 CE) represented another leap forward. Paper money spread globally, eventually becoming a common medium of exchange.

- Convenience: Lighter and more portable than metal coins.

- Flexibility: This could be issued in various denominations to suit different transaction sizes.

- Economic Expansion: Facilitated larger-scale trade and commerce.

The Gold Standard and Fiat Money

The gold standard, which linked currency value directly to gold, provided a stable foundation for international trade. However, it also imposed constraints on monetary policy and economic growth.

- Fixed Exchange Rates: Stabilized international trade by providing predictable currency values.

- Monetary Constraints: Limited the ability of governments to respond to economic crises due to the fixed supply of gold.

In the 20th century, the transition to fiat money—currency without intrinsic value but established as legal tender by government decree—allowed for greater flexibility in monetary policy.

- Government Control: Central banks could manage the money supply to stabilize the economy.

- Inflation Management: Provided tools to combat inflation and deflation.

The Functions of Money

Money serves several critical functions in the economy:

1. Medium of Exchange: Facilitates trade by eliminating the inefficiencies of barter.

2. Unit of Account: Provides a common measure of value, making it easier to compare prices and value goods and services.

3. Store of Value: Allows individuals and businesses to save and store wealth for future use.

4. Standard of Deferred Payment: Enables the settlement of debts and future payments, essential for credit and finance.

Modern Monetary Systems

Central Banking

Central banks play a crucial role in managing money supply and ensuring economic stability. They use various tools, including interest rates, reserve requirements, and open market operations, to influence economic activity.

- Monetary Policy: Central banks control inflation, manage employment levels, and stabilize the financial system.

- Financial Supervision: Regulate and supervise financial institutions to ensure stability and protect depositors.

- Currency Issuance: Central banks are responsible for issuing and managing national currency.

Digital and Cryptocurrencies

The advent of digital currencies and cryptocurrencies has introduced new dimensions to the science of money.

- Digital Currencies: Central bank digital currencies (CBDCs) and other forms of digital money offer greater efficiency and accessibility.

- Cryptocurrencies: Decentralized digital currencies like Bitcoin and Ethereum operate on blockchain technology, providing alternative means of exchange and store of value.

- Regulatory Challenges: The rise of digital and cryptocurrencies poses regulatory and security challenges that need to be addressed.

The Interplay of Money, Economics, and Society

The science of money is deeply intertwined with economics and societal development. Money influences economic activity, wealth distribution, and social structures.

- Economic Growth: Adequate money supply and sound monetary policy are crucial for sustainable economic growth.

- Income Inequality: The distribution of money affects income inequality and social mobility.

- Behavioral Economics: Understanding how people perceive and use money provides insights into economic behavior and decision-making.

The science of money encompasses a wide range of concepts, from its historical evolution and fundamental functions to the complexities of modern monetary systems. By exploring the intricate relationship between money, economics, and society, we gain a deeper understanding of the forces that drive economic activity and influence our daily lives. This foundational knowledge sets the stage for further exploration into the various aspects of money and its pivotal role in shaping the modern world.

WHY THE SCIENCE OF MONEY IS IMPERATIVE IN TODAY'S WORLD

The science of money, encompassing its creation, management, and implications, is a cornerstone of modern economies. Understanding the intricacies of money is crucial for individuals, businesses, and governments alike. In today's complex and interconnected world, where financial decisions and economic policies impact every aspect of life, the science of money provides the foundation for economic stability, growth, and prosperity. This chapter explores why a comprehensive understanding of money is essential in contemporary society and highlights the key areas where this knowledge is particularly critical.

Financial Literacy and Personal Well-being

Empowering Individuals

Financial literacy, or the understanding of financial principles and concepts, is vital for personal well-being. It enables individuals to make informed decisions about budgeting, saving, investing, and borrowing.

- Budgeting: Effective money management requires the ability to create and adhere to a budget, ensuring that income covers expenses and allows for savings.

- Saving and Investing: Understanding the principles of saving and investing helps individuals build wealth over time and achieve financial goals such as buying a home, funding education, or retiring comfortably.

- Debt Management: Knowledge of interest rates, credit scores, and repayment strategies helps individuals avoid excessive debt and manage existing obligations effectively.

Enhancing Financial Security

Financial literacy contributes to financial security, reducing stress and enhancing quality of life.

- Emergency Funds: Knowledge of the importance of having an emergency fund helps individuals prepare for unexpected expenses and avoid financial crises.

- Retirement Planning: Understanding retirement planning options, such as 401(k)s, IRAs, and pensions, ensures that individuals can secure their financial future.

- Insurance: Awareness of various insurance products, including health, life, and property insurance, protects against significant financial losses due to unforeseen events.

Business Success and Economic Growth

Informed Business Decisions

For businesses, a deep understanding of money and finance is essential for making strategic decisions that drive growth and profitability.

- Financial Planning: Businesses need to create detailed financial plans, including revenue forecasts, expense budgets, and capital investment plans, to ensure sustainable growth.

- Cost Management: Effective cost management strategies help businesses control expenses, maximize profits, and remain competitive in the market.

- Investment Strategies: Knowledge of different investment options and their associated risks and returns enables businesses to allocate resources efficiently and generate higher returns.

Access to Capital

Understanding money is crucial for businesses seeking to raise capital for expansion and innovation.

- Funding Options: Businesses must navigate various funding options, including loans, equity financing, and venture capital, to secure the necessary resources for growth.

- Financial Statements: Accurate financial statements and reports are essential for attracting investors and securing financing. They provide a clear picture of a company's financial health and future prospects.

- Risk Management: Effective risk management practices, such as hedging and diversification, protect businesses from financial losses and enhance long-term stability.

Government Policy and Economic Stability

Monetary Policy

Governments and central banks use monetary policy to manage the economy and ensure stability.

- Inflation Control: Understanding how to control inflation through interest rates and money supply adjustments is critical for maintaining the purchasing power of money and economic stability.

- Employment Levels: Monetary policy tools are used to influence employment levels by stimulating or cooling economic activity as needed.

- Economic Growth: By managing interest rates and liquidity, governments can foster an environment conducive to economic growth and development.

Fiscal Policy

Fiscal policy, involving government spending and taxation, is another critical area where the science of money plays a significant role.

- Budget Deficits and Surpluses: Understanding the implications of budget deficits and surpluses helps governments make informed decisions about public spending and taxation.

- Public Debt Management: Effective management of public debt ensures that governments can meet their obligations without compromising economic stability.

- Social Programs: Knowledge of fiscal policy is essential for designing and funding social programs that promote economic equality and social welfare.

Global Interconnectedness and Trade

International Trade and Finance

In an increasingly globalized world, understanding the science of money is essential for managing international trade and finance.

- Exchange Rates: Knowledge of exchange rate mechanisms and their impact on trade balances and economic competitiveness is crucial for businesses and governments.

- Trade Agreements: Understanding the financial implications of trade agreements helps countries negotiate favorable terms and promote economic growth.

- Cross-Border Investments: Awareness of international investment opportunities and risks enables businesses and investors to diversify their portfolios and enhance returns.

Economic Interdependence

Global economic interdependence means that financial decisions in one country can have far-reaching effects on others.

- Financial Crises: Understanding the causes and consequences of financial crises, such as the 2008 global financial crisis, helps countries implement policies to prevent and mitigate similar events.

- Economic Policies: Coordination of economic policies among countries is essential for addressing global challenges such as climate change, poverty, and economic inequality.

Technological Advancements and Innovation

Digital Currencies and Blockchain

The advent of digital currencies and blockchain technology is revolutionizing the financial landscape.

- Cryptocurrencies: Understanding the principles and implications of cryptocurrencies, such as Bitcoin and

Ethereum, is essential for navigating the evolving financial ecosystem.

- Blockchain: Knowledge of blockchain technology and its applications in finance, such as smart contracts and decentralized finance (DeFi), is critical for staying ahead in the innovation curve.

Financial Technology (Fintech)

Fintech innovations are transforming how financial services are delivered and accessed.

- Mobile Banking: Understanding mobile banking and payment systems enhances financial inclusion and accessibility.

- Robo-Advisors: Awareness of robo-advisors and automated investment platforms helps individuals and businesses make informed investment decisions.

- Data Analytics: Leveraging data analytics and artificial intelligence in finance improves decision-making, risk management, and customer service.

Ethical and Social Implications

Income Inequality

Understanding the science of money helps address issues of income inequality and promote economic justice.

- Wealth Distribution: Analyzing the factors that contribute to wealth distribution and implementing policies to reduce income disparity enhances social cohesion and stability.

- Living Standards: Ensuring fair wages and access to financial resources improves living standards and economic opportunities for all.

Sustainable Development

Knowledge of sustainable finance and investment practices promotes environmentally and socially responsible economic growth.

- Green Finance: Understanding the principles of green finance and sustainable investing supports efforts to combat climate change and promote environmental sustainability.

- Corporate Social Responsibility: Encouraging businesses to adopt ethical practices and contribute positively to society enhances corporate reputation and long-term success.

Conclusion

The science of money is imperative in today's world due to its profound impact on personal well-being, business success, government policy, global trade, technological innovation, and social equity. By understanding the principles and applications of money, individuals, businesses, and governments can make informed decisions that promote financial stability, economic growth, and social welfare. As the financial landscape continues to evolve, staying informed and adaptable will be essential for navigating the complexities of the modern economy and ensuring a prosperous future for all.

DR. MAXWELL SHIMBA

CHAPTER 1

INTRODUCTION TO MONEY

The Evolution of Money

Money, in its various forms, has been a cornerstone of human civilization. It has evolved from simple barter systems to complex financial instruments, reflecting the changing needs and sophistication of societies.

The Barter System

Before the advent of money, people relied on bartering to facilitate trade. Barter involves the direct exchange of goods and services without a standardized medium of exchange. For example, a farmer might trade a bushel of wheat for a craftsman's pottery. While bartering allowed for trade, it had significant limitations:

- Double Coincidence of Wants: Both parties in a barter trade must have what the other desires.

- Lack of Standardization: There is no common measure of value, making it difficult to compare the worth of different goods and services.

- Indivisibility of Goods: Some goods cannot be easily divided to facilitate smaller transactions.

Emergence of Commodity Money

To overcome the inefficiencies of barter, early societies began using commodity money—items that had intrinsic value and were widely accepted in trade. Examples include:

- Shells: Used in various cultures, such as the cowrie shells in Africa and Asia.

- Precious Metals: Gold, silver, and copper became popular due to their durability, divisibility, and intrinsic value.

- Livestock: In agricultural societies, cattle and other livestock served as a medium of exchange.

Commodity money provided a more efficient means of trade, allowing for a standard measure of value and the ability to store wealth.

The Invention of Coins

Around 600 BCE, the Lydians in present-day Turkey began minting the first coins. Coins were made from precious metals and stamped with symbols to signify their authenticity and value. This innovation had several advantages:

- Uniformity: Coins had a standard weight and purity, making them widely accepted.

- Portability: Coins were easier to carry and use in trade than bulky commodities.

- Durability: Precious metals resisted wear and could be stored for long periods without losing value.

The use of coins spread rapidly across the ancient world, facilitating trade and commerce.

Introduction of Paper Money

The next significant evolution in money came with the introduction of paper money. China was the first to use paper currency during the Tang Dynasty (618–907 CE), and its usage expanded during the Song Dynasty (960–1279 CE). Paper money offered several benefits:

- Convenience: Lighter and easier to transport than metal coins.

- Flexibility: This could be issued in various denominations to suit different transaction sizes.

- Economic Expansion: Facilitated larger-scale trade and commerce.

Europe adopted paper money much later, with the first European banknotes issued by the Stockholms Banco in Sweden in 1661.

Modern Money and Digital Transactions

In the 20th and 21st centuries, money continued to evolve with the advent of digital transactions and electronic banking. Modern money includes:

- Fiat Currency: Government-issued money that is not backed by a physical commodity but by the trust and authority of the issuing government.

- Digital Currency: Electronic forms of money used for online transactions. This includes both traditional bank accounts and newer forms such as cryptocurrencies.

- Cryptocurrencies: Decentralized digital currencies like Bitcoin, which use blockchain technology to secure transactions and control the creation of new units.

The Role of Money as a Medium of Exchange

Money serves several crucial functions in an economy:

- Medium of Exchange: Facilitates trade by eliminating the inefficiencies of barter.

- Unit of Account: Provides a standard measure of value, making it easier to compare prices and value goods and services.

- Store of Value: Allows individuals and businesses to save and store wealth for future use.

- Standard of Deferred Payment: Enables the settlement of debts and future payments, essential for credit and finance.

Conclusion

The journey of money from barter to digital currencies reflects humanity's ongoing quest for more efficient and effective means of trade. Each innovation in the history of money has addressed specific limitations of previous systems, paving the way for the complex financial systems we rely on today. As we move forward, the future of money promises to bring even more transformative changes, driven by technological advancements and changing economic landscapes.

CHAPTER 02

THE ECONOMICS OF MONEY

Understanding the Economic Principles Behind Money

Money is not just a medium of exchange; it is also a critical element in the economic system, influencing various aspects of the economy. This chapter delves into the fundamental economic principles that underpin the concept of money, including supply and demand, inflation, and the impact of monetary policy.

Supply and Demand

The Law of Supply and Demand

At the heart of economic theory lies the law of supply and demand, which dictates that the price of a good or service is determined by the relationship between its availability (supply) and the desire of buyers (demand).

- Supply: Refers to the total amount of a specific good or service that is available to consumers. In the context of money, supply can be thought of as the total amount of money in circulation within an economy.

- Demand: Refers to consumers' willingness and ability to purchase a good or service. In monetary terms, demand for money reflects the desire to hold money for transactions, savings, and investments.

The equilibrium price is reached when the quantity supplied equals the quantity demanded. For money, this equilibrium determines interest rates and the overall level of economic activity.

Money Supply

The money supply encompasses all the currency and other liquid instruments in a country's economy. It is typically categorized into several measures:

- M1: Includes physical currency, demand deposits, traveler's checks, and other checkable deposits.

- M2: Includes M1 plus savings deposits, money market mutual funds, and other time deposits.

Central banks, such as the Federal Reserve in the United States, play a crucial role in regulating the money supply through monetary policy tools.

Inflation

Definition and Causes

Inflation is the rate at which the general level of prices for goods and services rises, eroding purchasing power. Several factors can cause inflation:

- Demand-Pull Inflation: Occurs when demand for goods and services exceeds supply, driving prices up.

- Cost-Push Inflation: Happens when the costs of production increase, leading businesses to raise prices to maintain profit margins.

- Built-In Inflation: Arises from adaptive expectations, where workers demand higher wages to keep up with rising living costs, leading businesses to increase prices further.

Measuring Inflation

Inflation is commonly measured by indices such as:

- Consumer Price Index (CPI): Tracks the changes in prices of a basket of consumer goods and services.

- Producer Price Index (PPI): Measures the average change in selling prices received by domestic producers for their output.

Consequences of Inflation

While moderate inflation is a sign of a growing economy, high inflation can have adverse effects:

- Decreased Purchasing Power: Money buys fewer goods and services.

- Uncertainty: High inflation can create uncertainty, discouraging investment and savings.

- Redistribution of Wealth: Inflation can erode the value of money, impacting savers and those on fixed incomes more than debtors.

Monetary Policy

Role of Central Banks

Central banks are responsible for implementing monetary policy to control inflation, manage employment levels, and ensure economic stability. They use various tools to influence the money supply and interest rates.

Tools of Monetary Policy

1. Open Market Operations (OMO): The buying and selling of government securities in the open market to regulate the money supply. Purchasing securities injects money into the economy while selling securities withdraws money.

2. Interest Rates: Central banks set the benchmark interest rates, such as the federal funds rate, influencing borrowing costs and economic activity.

3. Reserve Requirements: Regulations on the minimum amount of reserves banks must hold against deposits. Lowering reserve requirements increases the money supply while raising them reduces it.

4. Quantitative Easing (QE): A non-traditional monetary policy tool used in times of economic crisis, where the central bank purchases long-term securities to increase the money supply and encourage lending and investment.

Impact of Monetary Policy

Monetary policy can have profound effects on the economy:

- Economic Growth: By influencing interest rates and the availability of credit, monetary policy can stimulate or cool down economic activity.

- Employment: Lower interest rates can boost business investment and consumer spending, leading to job creation. Conversely, higher rates can reduce inflation but may also slow down the economy and increase unemployment.

- Inflation Control: Central banks aim to keep inflation within a target range to maintain price stability, which is crucial for long-term economic planning and investment.

Conclusion

Understanding the economics of money is essential for grasping how financial systems operate and how economic policies impact everyday life. The interplay between supply and demand, inflation, and monetary policy shapes the economic landscape, influencing everything from individual purchasing power to global economic trends. As we move forward, the principles outlined in this chapter will continue to play a pivotal role in shaping the future of money and economic stability.

CHAPTER 03

THE SCIENCE OF SPENDING MONEY

Spending money is a fundamental aspect of human behavior that impacts both personal and economic well-being. Understanding the science behind spending involves examining psychological, sociological, and economic factors that influence how, why, and when we spend money. This chapter explores these dynamics and offers insights into making more informed spending decisions.

Psychological Factors Influencing Spending

Emotional Spending

Emotions play a significant role in spending behavior. People often spend money to cope with emotions such as stress, sadness, or boredom.

- Retail Therapy: Shopping to improve mood or alleviate stress is common, but it can lead to impulsive purchases and financial strain.

- Hedonic Consumption: Spending on experiences or items that provide pleasure and enjoyment, such as vacations or luxury goods.

Cognitive Biases

Cognitive biases can distort spending decisions, leading to suboptimal financial outcomes.

- Anchoring Effect: Relying heavily on the first piece of information encountered (the anchor) when making decisions. For example, seeing a high initial price can make a discounted price seem more attractive.

- Loss Aversion: The tendency to prefer avoiding losses over acquiring equivalent gains. This can lead to overvaluing items already owned and making suboptimal financial choices.

- Present Bias: The preference for immediate rewards over future benefits, leading to impulsive spending and insufficient saving.

Social Influences

Social factors, including peer pressure and social norms, significantly impact spending behavior.

- Keeping Up with the Joneses: The desire to match the spending patterns of peers or social groups can drive unnecessary purchases and financial strain.

- Social Proof: The influence of others' behavior on one's own spending decisions. Seeing others spend on certain items can create a perception of necessity or desirability.

Economic Principles and Spending

Utility and Satisfaction

In economics, utility refers to the satisfaction or happiness derived from consuming goods and services.

- Diminishing Marginal Utility: The principle that the additional satisfaction gained from consuming one more unit of a good or service decreases as consumption increases. This helps explain why people diversify their spending rather than continually purchasing the same items.

- Opportunity Cost: The cost of forgoing the next best alternative when making a decision. Understanding opportunity costs can lead to more mindful spending choices.

Budgeting and Financial Planning

Effective financial planning and budgeting are essential for managing spending and achieving financial goals.

- Budgeting: Creating a detailed plan for how to spend and save money. A budget helps track expenses, prioritize needs over wants, and avoid overspending.

- Financial Goals: Setting short-term and long-term financial goals provides direction and motivation for disciplined spending and saving.

Behavioral Economics

Behavioral economics combines insights from psychology and economics to understand how people make financial decisions.

- Nudge Theory: Proposes subtle interventions to encourage better financial behaviors without restricting freedom of choice. Examples include automatic enrollment in retirement plans or setting default options for savings.

- Mental Accounting: The tendency to categorize and treat money differently based on its source or intended use. Recognizing this can help individuals manage their finances more effectively.

The Role of Marketing and Advertising

Influence of Marketing

Marketing and advertising are designed to influence consumer behavior and drive spending.

- Persuasion Techniques: Advertisers use techniques such as scarcity (limited-time offers), social proof (testimonials), and emotional appeals to influence purchasing decisions.

- Brand Loyalty: Building strong brand loyalty encourages repeat purchases and increases customer lifetime value.

Consumer Awareness

Being aware of marketing tactics can help consumers make more informed spending decisions.

- Critical Thinking: Evaluating advertisements and marketing messages critically to distinguish between genuine value and manipulative tactics.

- Informed Choices: Researching products and comparing options to ensure purchases meet needs and provide value for money.

Strategies for Smart Spending

Needs vs. Wants

Distinguishing between needs and wants is crucial for managing spending effectively.

- Needs: Essential items required for survival and well-being, such as food, shelter, and healthcare.

- Wants: Non-essential items that provide comfort and pleasure but are not necessary for basic functioning.

Prioritizing Value

Focusing on value rather than cost alone can lead to more satisfying and sustainable spending habits.

- Quality over Quantity: Investing in high-quality items that last longer and provide greater satisfaction.

- Cost-Benefit Analysis: Assessing the benefits relative to the costs of a purchase to determine its overall value.

Avoiding Impulsive Spending

Implementing strategies to control impulsive spending can help maintain financial stability.

- Cooling-Off Period: Waiting for a set period before making a purchase decision to avoid impulsive buying.

- Shopping Lists: Using lists to stay focused on necessary items and avoid unplanned purchases.

Leveraging Technology

Technology offers tools and resources to support smart spending and financial management.

- Budgeting Apps: Apps like Mint, YNAB (You Need a Budget), and PocketGuard help track expenses, set budgets, and monitor financial goals.

- Price Comparison Tools: Online tools and apps that compare prices across different retailers to find the best deals.

Impact of Spending on Personal and Economic Well-Being

Personal Financial Health

Responsible spending is critical for maintaining personal financial health and achieving long-term financial goals.

- Savings and Investments: Prioritizing saving and investing can provide financial security and enable wealth accumulation.

- Debt Management: Avoiding excessive debt and managing existing debt responsibly to maintain financial stability.

Economic Growth

Consumer spending is a major driver of economic growth, influencing business revenue, employment, and overall economic activity.

- Consumption Patterns: Changes in consumer spending patterns can signal shifts in economic conditions and impact business strategies.

- Economic Cycles: Consumer spending tends to fluctuate with economic cycles, affecting demand for goods and services and overall economic performance.

Conclusion

The science of spending money encompasses a wide range of psychological, economic, and social factors. By understanding these influences and implementing strategies for smart spending, individuals can enhance their financial well-being and contribute to broader economic stability. As technology and consumer behavior continue to evolve, staying informed and adaptable will be key to making sound financial decisions in the future.

CHAPTER 04

THE SCIENCE OF DEBT

Debt is a pervasive element of modern financial systems, impacting individuals, businesses, and governments. Understanding the science of debt involves exploring its types, purposes, psychological and economic impacts, and strategies for effective management. This chapter comprehensively overviews debt and its role in financial stability and growth.

Types of Debt

Personal Debt

Personal debt refers to liabilities incurred by individuals or households.

- Credit Card Debt: Unsecured debt accumulated through the use of credit cards, often characterized by high interest rates.

- Personal Loans: Unsecured or secured loans taken out for various purposes, such as consolidating debt, covering emergency expenses, or making large purchases.

- Mortgages: Secured loans used to purchase real estate, with the property serving as collateral.

- Student Loans: Borrowed funds specifically intended to finance education, often with favorable terms compared to other types of personal debt.

Business Debt

Business debt refers to liabilities incurred by companies to finance operations, expansion, and other activities.

- Commercial Loans: Loans provided by banks or other financial institutions to businesses, often used for working capital or capital expenditures.

- Corporate Bonds: Debt securities issued by corporations to raise capital from investors, with a promise to pay back the principal along with interest.

- Lines of Credit: Flexible borrowing options that allow businesses to access funds up to a certain limit as needed.

Government Debt

Government debt refers to the liabilities incurred by governments to finance public expenditures.

- Sovereign Bonds: Debt securities issued by national governments, often denominated in the country's own currency or a foreign currency.

- Municipal Bonds: Bonds issued by local governments or municipalities to finance public projects, such as infrastructure improvements and schools.

- Treasury Securities: Government debt instruments issued by the treasury department, including Treasury bills, notes, and bonds.

Purposes of Debt

Consumption Smoothing

Debt allows individuals and households to smooth consumption over time, enabling them to make significant purchases or cover unexpected expenses without immediate financial strain.

Investment and Growth

Debt provides businesses and governments with the necessary capital to invest in projects, infrastructure, and other activities that promote growth and development.

- Capital Expenditures: Businesses use debt to finance long-term investments, such as new equipment, technology, and facilities.

- Public Investment: Governments borrow to fund public goods and services, such as transportation infrastructure, education, and healthcare.

Risk Management

Debt can be used as a tool for managing financial risks, such as hedging against fluctuations in cash flow or interest rates.

- Leverage: Businesses may use debt to leverage their operations, amplifying potential returns on investment while managing risk.

- Insurance: Households may incur debt to cover unexpected emergencies, such as medical expenses or property damage.

Psychological Factors Influencing Debt

Debt Aversion

Debt aversion refers to the reluctance or unwillingness to incur debt, often driven by fear of financial risk or a desire to avoid obligations.

- Emotional Impact: High levels of debt can cause stress, anxiety, and other negative emotions.

- Cultural Factors: Societal attitudes towards debt can influence individual willingness to borrow.

Debt Acceptance

Conversely, some individuals and entities view debt as a useful financial tool and are more willing to incur and manage it.

- Financial Literacy: Understanding the benefits and risks of debt can lead to more informed borrowing decisions.

- Rational Borrowing: When used strategically, debt can enhance financial well-being and growth opportunities.

Economic Principles of Debt

Cost of Borrowing

The cost of borrowing, or interest rate, is a critical factor in the decision to take on debt.

- Interest Rates: The cost of borrowing varies depending on the type of debt, the borrower's creditworthiness, and market conditions.

- Credit Risk: Lenders assess the risk of default when determining interest rates, with higher-risk borrowers facing higher rates.

Debt Sustainability

Debt sustainability refers to the ability of a borrower to meet debt obligations without resorting to excessive borrowing or compromising financial stability.

- Debt-to-Income Ratio: A measure of an individual's or household's debt relative to their income, used to assess their ability to manage debt.

- Debt-to-GDP Ratio: A measure of a government's debt relative to its gross domestic product (GDP), used to assess the sustainability of public debt.

Impact of Debt on Financial Stability

Positive Impacts

When managed responsibly, debt can have several positive impacts on financial stability and growth.

- Economic Growth: Access to credit can stimulate investment, consumption, and economic activity.

- Financial Inclusion: Debt enables individuals and businesses to access capital and participate in the economy.

Negative Impacts

Excessive or poorly managed debt can lead to financial instability and economic downturns.

- Debt Overhang: High levels of debt can constrain borrowing and investment, leading to slower economic growth.

- Default Risk: The risk of default can lead to financial crises, affecting lenders, borrowers, and the broader economy.

- Debt Traps: Continuous borrowing to service existing debt can lead to a cycle of increasing debt and financial distress.

Strategies for Managing Debt

Personal Debt Management

- Budgeting: Creating and adhering to a budget helps individuals manage income and expenses, reducing the need for unnecessary borrowing.

- Debt Repayment Plans: Developing a structured plan for paying off debt, prioritizing high-interest debt, and setting realistic goals.

- Credit Counseling: Seeking professional advice and assistance to manage debt effectively.

Business Debt Management

- Cash Flow Management: Businesses should monitor and manage cash flow to ensure they can meet debt obligations.

- Diversified Financing: Using a mix of debt and equity financing to reduce financial risk and maintain flexibility.

- Risk Assessment: Conducting thorough risk assessments before taking on new debt to ensure it aligns with business goals and financial capacity.

Government Debt Management

- Fiscal Discipline: Governments should adopt sound fiscal policies, maintaining a balance between revenue and expenditure.

- Debt Issuance Strategy: Implementing a strategic approach to issuing debt, considering market conditions and long-term sustainability.

- Debt Restructuring: In cases of financial distress, restructuring debt can provide relief and restore stability.

Conclusion

The science of debt encompasses a wide range of psychological, economic, and strategic considerations. Understanding the various types of debt, their purposes, and the factors influencing borrowing decisions is essential for managing debt effectively and maintaining financial stability. By adopting responsible borrowing practices and implementing effective debt management strategies, individuals, businesses, and governments can harness the benefits of debt while minimizing its risks. As financial systems continue to evolve, ongoing education and awareness will be crucial for navigating the complexities of debt in the modern economy.

CHAPTER 05

THE SCIENCE OF GENERATING INCOME

Generating income is a fundamental aspect of economic activity and financial stability for individuals, businesses, and governments. Understanding the science of generating income involves exploring various sources, strategies, and economic principles that drive income generation. This chapter delves into the methods and factors influencing the ability to generate income effectively and sustainably.

Sources of Income

Personal Income

Personal income is the earnings received by individuals from various sources. Key sources of personal income include:

- Employment Income: Wages, salaries, bonuses, and other compensation received from working.

- Business Income: Earnings from owning and operating a business or self-employment.

- Investment Income: Returns from investments, including interest, dividends, capital gains, and rental income.

- Transfer Payments: Government benefits and social security payments, such as unemployment benefits, pensions, and welfare.

Business Income

Business income is the revenue generated by companies from their operations. Major sources include:

- Sales Revenue: Income from selling goods and services to customers.

- Service Fees: Earnings from providing services, such as consulting, maintenance, and professional services.

- Licensing and Royalties: Income from licensing intellectual property, patents, and trademarks.

- Investment Income: Returns from business investments, such as dividends, interest, and capital gains.

Government Income

Governments generate income to fund public services and infrastructure. Key sources include:

- Taxes: Income, sales, property, and corporate taxes collected from individuals and businesses.

- Fees and Charges: Revenue from fees for services, such as permits, licenses, and tolls.

- Fines and Penalties: Income from fines and penalties imposed for legal and regulatory violations.

- Investment Income: Returns from government investments in financial assets and state-owned enterprises.

Strategies for Generating Personal Income

Employment Strategies

- Education and Skills Development: Investing in education and acquiring new skills to enhance employability and earning potential.

- Career Advancement: Seeking promotions, taking on additional responsibilities, and pursuing opportunities for professional growth.

- Networking: Building a professional network to access job opportunities and career advice.

Entrepreneurial Strategies

- Starting a Business: Identifying market opportunities, creating a business plan, and launching a business to generate income.

- Freelancing and Gig Economy: Offering skills and services on a freelance basis or participating in the gig economy for additional income.

- Passive Income Streams: Creating sources of passive income, such as rental properties, royalties, or online content monetization.

Investment Strategies

- Diversification: Investing in a diversified portfolio of assets, including stocks, bonds, real estate, and alternative investments, to generate returns and reduce risk.

- Dividend Investing: Investing in dividend-paying stocks to receive regular income distributions.

- Interest-Bearing Accounts: Placing funds in savings accounts, certificates of deposit, or bonds to earn interest income.

Strategies for Generating Business Income

Sales and Marketing

- Market Research: Conducting market research to understand customer needs and preferences, identify target markets, and develop effective marketing strategies.

- Product Development: Innovating and developing new products or improving existing ones to meet customer demand and generate sales.

- Sales Channels: Utilizing multiple sales channels, such as online platforms, retail stores, and direct sales, to reach a broader customer base.

Cost Management

- Efficiency Improvements: Streamlining operations and processes to reduce costs and increase profitability.

- Supplier Negotiations: Negotiating favorable terms with suppliers to reduce input costs and improve margins.

- Lean Management: Implementing lean management practices to eliminate waste and optimize resource utilization.

Strategic Partnerships

- Joint Ventures: Forming joint ventures with other businesses to share resources, expertise, and market access.

- Strategic Alliances: Establishing strategic alliances with complementary businesses to expand market reach and enhance competitiveness.

- Franchising: Offering franchising opportunities to expand business operations and generate franchise fees and royalties.

Economic Principles Influencing Income Generation

Supply and Demand

The principles of supply and demand play a crucial role in income generation. The price and quantity of goods and services sold are determined by the interaction of supply and demand in the market.

- Elasticity: Understanding the price elasticity of demand for products and services helps businesses set pricing strategies to maximize revenue.

- Market Equilibrium: Achieving market equilibrium, where supply equals demand, ensures stable prices and consistent sales.

Productivity

Productivity, or the efficiency with which inputs are converted into outputs, directly impacts income generation.

- Labor Productivity: Enhancing labor productivity through training, technology, and efficient work practices increases output and income.

- Capital Productivity: Investing in capital assets, such as machinery and technology, improves productivity and generates higher income.

Economic Cycles

Economic cycles, including periods of expansion and contraction, influence income generation.

- Expansion: During economic expansion, businesses experience increased demand, higher sales, and greater income.

- Recession: In times of recession, demand may decline, leading to reduced income and the need for cost-cutting measures.

Technological Advancements and Income Generation

Automation and AI

Automation and artificial intelligence (AI) are transforming the way income is generated by enhancing productivity and creating new opportunities.

- Process Automation: Automating repetitive tasks and processes reduces costs and increases efficiency, contributing to higher income.

- AI-Driven Insights: Utilizing AI and data analytics to gain insights into customer behavior, market trends, and operational efficiencies, driving better decision-making and income generation.

Digital Platforms

Digital platforms offer new avenues for income generation through online sales, services, and content creation.

- E-Commerce: Leveraging e-commerce platforms to reach a global customer base and generate sales.

- Online Services: Providing online services, such as consulting, coaching, and digital products, to generate income.

- Content Monetization: Creating and monetizing digital content through advertising, subscriptions, and affiliate marketing.

Challenges in Income Generation

Market Competition

Intense competition in the market can impact income generation by affecting pricing, market share, and profitability.

- Competitive Strategies: Develop unique value propositions, differentiation strategies, and competitive pricing to stay ahead of competitors.

Economic Uncertainty

Economic uncertainty, including fluctuations in interest rates, inflation, and geopolitical events, can affect income generation.

- Risk Management: Implementing risk management strategies, such as diversification and hedging, to mitigate the impact of economic uncertainty.

Regulatory Environment

Changes in regulations and compliance requirements can impact income generation for businesses and individuals.

- Compliance: Staying informed about regulatory changes and ensuring compliance to avoid legal issues and potential financial penalties.

Conclusion

The science of generating income involves understanding various sources, strategies, and economic principles that drive income generation. By leveraging personal skills, entrepreneurial ventures, investments, and technological advancements, individuals and businesses can enhance their ability to generate income effectively and sustainably. Navigating challenges such as market competition, economic uncertainty, and regulatory changes requires informed decision-making and strategic planning. As the economic landscape continues to evolve, staying adaptable and proactive will be key to maximizing income generation and achieving financial success.

CHAPTER 06

THE SCIENCE OF CREATING WEALTH

Wealth creation is the process of generating assets and resources that increase in value over time, providing financial security and enabling individuals, businesses, and societies to achieve their goals. Understanding the science behind creating wealth involves examining the principles, strategies, and behaviors that contribute to accumulating and growing wealth. This chapter explores various approaches to wealth creation, the factors influencing wealth accumulation, and the importance of financial literacy and disciplined practices.

Principles of Wealth Creation

The Power of Compound Interest

Compound interest is one of the most powerful principles in wealth creation. It involves earning interest on both the initial principal and the accumulated interest from previous periods.

- Growth Over Time: Compound interest allows investments to grow exponentially over time, emphasizing the importance of starting early.

- Reinvestment: Continuously reinvesting earnings accelerates the wealth creation process, leading to substantial growth in assets.

Diversification

Diversification involves spreading investments across various asset classes to reduce risk and increase potential returns.

- Risk Management: By diversifying, investors can mitigate the impact of poor performance in any single asset class.

- Balanced Portfolio: A well-diversified portfolio includes a mix of stocks, bonds, real estate, and other investments, providing stability and growth potential.

Leverage

Leverage involves using borrowed capital to increase the potential return on investment.

- Amplifying Returns: When used wisely, leverage can amplify returns and accelerate wealth creation.

- Risk Considerations: Leverage also increases risk, so it must be managed carefully to avoid significant losses.

Strategies for Creating Wealth

Investing in Financial Markets

Investing in financial markets is a common strategy for creating wealth.

- Stock Market: Investing in stocks offers the potential for high returns through capital appreciation and dividends. Long-term investment in diversified stocks can build substantial wealth.

- Bonds: Bonds provide steady income through interest payments and are generally less volatile than stocks. Including bonds in a portfolio helps balance risk and return.

- Mutual Funds and ETFs: Mutual funds and exchange-traded funds (ETFs) offer diversification and professional management, making them accessible options for individual investors.

Real Estate Investment

Real estate is a tangible asset that can generate wealth through appreciation, rental income, and tax benefits.

- Property Appreciation: Real estate tends to appreciate over time, providing capital gains when sold.

- Rental Income: Owning rental properties generates regular income and can cover mortgage payments, maintenance, and other expenses.

- Leverage Opportunities: Real estate allows for significant leverage, enabling investors to purchase properties with a relatively small initial investment.

Entrepreneurship

Starting and growing a business is a direct way to create wealth.

- Value Creation: Successful businesses create value by providing goods or services that meet market needs.

- Equity Ownership: Owning equity in a business allows entrepreneurs to benefit from the company's growth and profitability.

- Scalability: Businesses that can scale efficiently have the potential to generate substantial wealth.

Factors Influencing Wealth Accumulation

Income Generation

Regular and increasing income is fundamental to accumulating wealth.

- Career Development: Pursuing higher education, acquiring skills, and advancing in one's career can lead to higher income and greater wealth accumulation.

- Multiple Income Streams: Diversifying income sources, such as through investments, side businesses, or passive income, enhances financial stability and growth.

Savings and Frugality

Saving a portion of income and practicing frugality are essential habits for wealth creation.

- Consistent Savings: Regularly setting aside a portion of income for savings builds a financial cushion and provides capital for investments.

- Living Below Means: Spending less than one earns allows for greater savings and investment opportunities.

Financial Literacy

Understanding financial concepts and strategies is crucial for making informed decisions and creating wealth.

- Education: Investing in financial education, such as reading books, taking courses, and seeking advice from financial professionals, enhances one's ability to manage and grow wealth.

- Informed Decisions: Financial literacy enables individuals to evaluate investment opportunities, manage debt, and plan for long-term financial goals.

Behaviors and Mindsets for Wealth Creation

Discipline and Consistency

Building wealth requires disciplined saving, investing, and spending habits.

- Regular Investing: Consistently investing a portion of income, regardless of market conditions, leads to significant wealth accumulation over time.

- Budgeting: Creating and sticking to a budget ensures that spending aligns with financial goals and priorities.

Long-Term Perspective

Adopting a long-term perspective is key to successful wealth creation.

- Patience: Wealth creation takes time, and staying invested through market fluctuations is crucial for long-term growth.

- Goal Setting: Setting clear, long-term financial goals provides direction and motivation for consistent wealth-building efforts.

Risk Management

Effective risk management protects wealth and ensures sustainable growth.

- Insurance: Adequate insurance coverage, such as health, life, and property insurance, mitigates financial risks and protects assets.

- Emergency Fund: Maintaining an emergency fund covers unexpected expenses and prevents the need to liquidate investments during market downturns.

The Role of Technology in Wealth Creation

Financial Technology (Fintech)

Fintech innovations provide tools and platforms that make wealth creation more accessible and efficient.

- Robo-Advisors: Automated investment platforms offer personalized portfolio management at lower costs, making investing accessible to more people.

- Mobile Banking: Mobile banking apps provide convenient access to financial services, enabling better money management and investment decisions.

Online Learning and Resources

The internet offers a wealth of information and resources for financial education and investment opportunities.

- Educational Platforms: Online courses, webinars, and financial blogs provide valuable knowledge and insights into wealth creation strategies.

- Investment Tools: Online tools and calculators help individuals plan and optimize their investment strategies.

Common Pitfalls in Wealth Creation

Overleveraging

Excessive use of leverage can lead to significant financial losses if investments do not perform as expected.

- Risk Assessment: Carefully assessing the risks and potential returns of leveraged investments is crucial to avoid overextending financially.

Market Timing

Attempting to time the market often leads to missed opportunities and suboptimal returns.

- Consistent Investing: Adopting a disciplined, long-term investment approach, such as dollar-cost averaging, helps mitigate the risks of market timing.

Lack of Diversification

Concentrating investments in a single asset class or sector increases vulnerability to market fluctuations.

- Portfolio Diversification: Spreading investments across various asset classes and sectors reduces risk and enhances long-term returns.

Conclusion

The science of creating wealth involves understanding and applying principles, strategies, and behaviors that promote the accumulation and growth of assets. By leveraging the power of compound interest, diversifying investments, and adopting disciplined financial habits, individuals and businesses can build substantial wealth over time. Financial literacy, long-term perspective, and effective risk management are essential components of successful wealth creation. As technology continues to evolve, it provides new tools and opportunities for accessing financial resources and making informed decisions. By avoiding common pitfalls and staying committed to wealth-building goals, anyone can achieve financial security and prosperity.

CHAPTER 07

THE SCIENCE OF MULTIPLYING WEALTH

Multiplying wealth goes beyond simply accumulating assets; it involves strategies and principles that enable wealth to grow exponentially. Understanding the science of multiplying wealth requires examining advanced investment techniques, leveraging opportunities, and adopting a disciplined approach to managing and growing assets. This chapter explores various methods to multiply wealth, the factors that influence exponential growth, and the importance of strategic planning and risk management.

Principles of Multiplying Wealth

Compound Interest and Reinvestment

Compound interest plays a pivotal role in multiplying wealth. It involves earning interest on both the principal and the accumulated interest from previous periods.

- Reinvestment Strategy: Continuously reinvesting earnings from investments, such as dividends, interest, or capital gains, accelerates wealth growth.

- Long-Term Perspective: The longer the investment period, the greater the exponential growth due to compounding.

Leverage

Leverage involves using borrowed capital to increase the potential return on investment. While it magnifies gains, it also increases risk.

- Real Estate: Using mortgages to acquire property can amplify returns through rental income and property appreciation.

- Margin Trading: Borrowing funds from a broker to trade financial assets can lead to significant gains, provided the investments perform well.

Diversification and Asset Allocation

Diversification spreads investments across various asset classes to reduce risk and enhance returns.

- Balanced Portfolio: A diversified portfolio includes a mix of stocks, bonds, real estate, and alternative investments, balancing risk and reward.

- Strategic Allocation: Adjusting asset allocation based on market conditions and financial goals optimizes portfolio performance.

Advanced Investment Techniques

Stock Market Strategies

Investing in the stock market offers the potential for high returns through various strategies.

- Growth Investing: Focusing on companies with high growth potential, even if their current earnings are low. These stocks often outperform the market over the long term.

- Value Investing: Identifying undervalued stocks with strong fundamentals, which are likely to increase in value as the market recognizes their true worth.

- Dividend Investing: Investing in companies that pay regular dividends, providing a steady income stream and potential for capital appreciation.

Real Estate Investment

Real estate remains a robust method for multiplying wealth through various strategies.

- Rental Properties: Generating income from rental properties provides steady cash flow and long-term appreciation.

- Flipping: Buying properties, renovating them, and selling at a higher price can yield significant short-term profits.

- Commercial Real Estate: Investing in commercial properties, such as office buildings and retail spaces, offers higher rental income and appreciation potential.

Alternative Investments

Exploring alternative investments can provide diversification and higher returns.

- Private Equity: Investing in private companies before they go public can offer substantial returns, though with higher risk.

- Hedge Funds: Participating in hedge funds allows for advanced investment strategies, such as short selling and derivatives, aiming for higher returns.

- Cryptocurrencies: Investing in digital currencies and blockchain projects presents high-risk, high-reward opportunities.

Leveraging Opportunities

Business Ownership and Entrepreneurship

Starting and growing a business can significantly multiply wealth.

- Scalability: Businesses that can scale efficiently have the potential to generate substantial income and increase in value.

- Innovation: Developing unique products or services that meet market needs can drive business growth and profitability.

Intellectual Property

Creating and monetizing intellectual property (IP) can generate ongoing income and appreciation.

- Patents and Trademarks: Licensing IP to other companies can provide royalty income.

- Content Creation: Producing valuable content, such as books, music, or digital media, can generate long-term revenue streams.

Franchising

Expanding a successful business through franchising can multiply wealth by leveraging the efforts of franchisees.

- Franchise Fees: Collecting upfront fees from franchisees provides immediate income.

- Royalty Payments: Ongoing royalties based on franchisee sales generate continuous income.

Strategic Planning for Wealth Multiplication

Financial Goals and Planning

Setting clear financial goals and developing a comprehensive plan is crucial for multiplying wealth.

- Short-Term and Long-Term Goals: Defining specific, measurable, achievable, relevant, and time-bound (SMART) goals guide investment strategies and decision-making.

- Regular Review: Continuously reviewing and adjusting the financial plan ensures alignment with changing market conditions and personal circumstances.

Tax Efficiency

Minimizing tax liabilities enhances wealth multiplication.

- Tax-Advantaged Accounts: Utilizing accounts such as IRAs, 401(k)s, and HSAs provides tax benefits and boosts investment growth.

- Tax Planning: Implementing strategies like tax-loss harvesting and deferring income can reduce tax burdens and increase net returns.

Risk Management

Diversification

Diversification reduces the impact of poor performance in any single investment, enhancing overall portfolio stability.

- Asset Classes: Investing across different asset classes, such as stocks, bonds, and real estate, mitigates risk.

- Geographical Diversification: Spreading investments across different regions and markets reduces exposure to local economic downturns.

Hedging

Hedging protects investments against adverse market movements.

- Options and Futures: Using options and futures contracts to hedge against price fluctuations in stocks, commodities, and currencies.

- Insurance: Purchasing insurance products, such as life and property insurance, protects against unforeseen events and financial losses.

Liquidity Management

Maintaining liquidity ensures the ability to meet short-term obligations and take advantage of investment opportunities.

- Emergency Fund: Keeping a portion of assets in liquid, low-risk investments provides a financial safety net.

- Cash Reserves: Holding cash reserves enables quick responses to market opportunities and emergencies.

Behavioral Finance and Wealth Multiplication

Discipline and Patience

Discipline and patience are essential for successful wealth multiplication.

- Consistent Investing: Regularly investing a portion of income, regardless of market conditions, leads to significant growth over time.

- Avoiding Emotional Decisions: Making investment decisions based on logic and analysis, rather than emotions, prevents costly mistakes.

Continuous Learning

Staying informed and continuously learning about financial markets, investment strategies, and economic trends enhances decision-making.

- Education: Engaging in financial education through books, courses, and seminars improves investment knowledge and skills.

- Advisory Services: Seeking advice from financial professionals provides valuable insights and guidance.

Technology and Wealth Multiplication

Financial Technology (Fintech)

Fintech innovations offer tools and platforms that make wealth multiplication more accessible and efficient.

- Automated Investing: Robo-advisors provide automated portfolio management, reducing costs and improving accessibility.

- Investment Apps: Mobile apps offer convenient access to investment opportunities, market data, and financial planning tools.

Data Analytics and AI

Data analytics and artificial intelligence (AI) enhance investment decision-making and portfolio management.

- Predictive Analytics: Using AI to analyze market trends and predict investment performance improves portfolio strategies.

- Automated Trading: Algorithmic trading systems execute trades based on predefined criteria, optimizing returns and minimizing risk.

Conclusion

The science of multiplying wealth involves leveraging advanced investment techniques, strategic planning, and disciplined financial behaviors to achieve exponential growth. By harnessing the power of compound interest, diversification, and leverage, individuals and businesses can significantly enhance their wealth over time. Effective risk management, continuous learning, and the use of technology further support the multiplication of wealth. As financial markets and economic conditions continue to evolve, staying informed and adaptable will be key to maximizing wealth and achieving long-term financial success.

CHAPTER 08

BANKING AND FINANCIAL INSTITUTIONS

The Role of Banks and Financial Institutions

Banks and financial institutions are the backbone of modern economies. They facilitate the flow of money, provide a safe place for savings, offer credit, and play a crucial role in the creation and management of money. This chapter explores their functions and significance in the financial system.

The Functions of Banks

Commercial Banks

Commercial banks are financial institutions that accept deposits, offer checking account services, make various loans, and provide basic financial products like certificates of deposit (CDs) and savings accounts.

1. Accepting Deposits: Banks provide a secure place for individuals and businesses to deposit their money. These deposits can be in the form of savings accounts, checking accounts, or fixed deposits.

2. Providing Loans: Banks lend money to individuals and businesses for various purposes, such as purchasing homes, funding business ventures, or personal needs. The interest earned on these loans is a primary source of income for banks.

3. Credit Creation: By lending out a portion of deposited funds, banks create credit. This process is central to the functioning of modern economies, as it increases the money supply and stimulates economic activity.

4. Payment and Settlement Services: Banks facilitate payments through services such as checks, electronic transfers, and credit/debit cards, making transactions efficient and secure.

5. Financial Advisory Services: Many banks offer financial planning, investment advisory, and wealth management services to help customers manage their finances effectively.

Central Banks

Central banks are national institutions responsible for managing a country's currency, money supply, and interest rates. The most well-known central bank is the Federal Reserve in the United States.

1. Monetary Policy: Central banks control the money supply and influence interest rates to stabilize the economy, aiming for low inflation and steady growth.

2. Banking Supervision: Central banks regulate and supervise commercial banks to ensure the stability and integrity of the financial system.

3. Lender of Last Resort: Central banks provide emergency funding to financial institutions in distress to prevent systemic failures and maintain financial stability.

4. Issuing Currency: Central banks have the exclusive authority to issue national currency, ensuring a stable and reliable supply of money.

Investment Banks

Investment banks assist companies in raising capital, advise on mergers and acquisitions, and provide other financial services tailored to corporations and governments.

1. Underwriting: Investment banks help companies issue new securities, such as stocks and bonds, by purchasing and reselling them to the public.

2. Advisory Services: They provide strategic advice on mergers, acquisitions, and other financial transactions, helping clients navigate complex financial landscapes.

3. Trading and Market Making: Investment banks engage in trading securities and act as market makers, providing liquidity and stability to financial markets.

Other Financial Institutions

In addition to banks, various other financial institutions play specialized roles in the economic system.

1. Credit Unions: Member-owned financial cooperatives that provide similar services to commercial banks but often at lower costs.

2. Insurance Companies: Provide risk management by offering insurance policies to protect against losses from various risks, such as accidents, health issues, and property damage.

3. Pension Funds: Manage retirement savings for individuals, investing contributions to ensure future payouts.

4. Mutual Funds: Pool money from many investors to buy a diversified portfolio of stocks, bonds, or other securities, offering professional management and risk diversification.

The Creation and Management of Money

Fractional Reserve Banking

Modern banking operates on a fractional reserve basis, where banks must keep only a fraction of their deposits as reserves. The rest can be loaned out, creating new money in the process. This system multiplies the money supply, amplifying the impact of central bank policies.

Money Creation Process

1. Deposits and Reserves: When a customer deposits money in a bank, a portion of that deposit is kept as reserves, while the rest is available for lending.

2. Lending: The bank lends out the remaining funds to borrowers. These borrowers then deposit the borrowed money into their bank accounts, and the cycle continues.

3. Money Multiplier: The process of repeated deposits and lending creates a money multiplier effect, where the total money supply is a multiple of the original deposits.

Managing Money Supply

Central banks use various tools to manage the money supply and ensure economic stability:

1. Open Market Operations (OMO): Buying and selling government securities to control the amount of money in circulation.

2. Interest Rates: Adjusting the benchmark interest rates to influence borrowing and spending.

3. Reserve Requirements: Changing the reserve ratio to increase or decrease the money that banks can lend out.

4. Quantitative Easing (QE): Purchasing long-term securities to inject liquidity into the economy during times of economic downturn.

The Importance of Financial Institutions

Financial institutions are essential for economic development and stability. They provide the necessary infrastructure for savings, investment, and the efficient allocation of resources. By facilitating transactions, managing risks, and offering credit, they support economic growth and development.

Conclusion

Banks and financial institutions are integral to the functioning of modern economies. Their roles in accepting deposits, providing loans, managing money supply, and offering financial services underpin the economic activities that drive growth and development. Understanding their functions and the mechanisms of money creation and management is crucial for appreciating the complexities of the financial system. As financial landscapes evolve, these institutions will continue to adapt, ensuring they remain vital components of the economic framework.

CHAPTER 09

THE SCIENCE OF WEALTH PROTECTION

Wealth protection is a crucial aspect of financial planning and management. It involves strategies and practices aimed at safeguarding accumulated wealth from various risks and uncertainties. Understanding the science of wealth protection is essential for ensuring long-term financial stability and security. This chapter explores the principles, strategies, and tools for protecting wealth, the importance of risk management, and the role of insurance and legal structures in preserving assets.

Principles of Wealth Protection

Risk Management

Effective risk management is the foundation of wealth protection. It involves identifying, assessing, and mitigating potential risks that could negatively impact wealth.

- Risk Assessment: Evaluating potential threats to wealth, such as market volatility, economic downturns, legal liabilities, and personal emergencies.

- Risk Mitigation: Implementing strategies to minimize the impact of identified risks, such as diversification, insurance, and contingency planning.

Diversification

Diversification is a key strategy for reducing risk and protecting wealth. It involves spreading investments across various asset classes and sectors to minimize the impact of poor performance in any single investment.

- Asset Classes: Investing in a mix of stocks, bonds, real estate, and alternative investments to balance risk and return.

- Geographic Diversification: Spreading investments across different regions and markets to reduce exposure to local economic downturns.

Strategies for Wealth Protection

Asset Allocation

Strategic asset allocation is essential for maintaining a balanced and resilient investment portfolio.

- Rebalancing: Regularly adjusting the allocation of assets to maintain the desired risk profile and investment objectives.

- Risk Tolerance: Aligning asset allocation with individual risk tolerance, financial goals, and time horizon.

Insurance

Insurance is a vital tool for protecting wealth from unexpected events and financial losses.

- Life Insurance: Provides financial security for dependents in the event of the policyholder's death, ensuring that their needs are met.

- Health Insurance: Covers medical expenses, protecting against the financial burden of illness or injury.

- Property Insurance: Protects against damage or loss of physical assets, such as homes, vehicles, and personal property.

- Liability Insurance: Shields against legal liabilities and potential lawsuits, covering legal fees and damages.

Legal Structures

Establishing appropriate legal structures can help protect wealth from creditors, legal disputes, and other risks.

- Trusts: Legal arrangements that hold assets on behalf of beneficiaries, providing protection from creditors and tax benefits.

- Limited Liability Companies (LLCs): Business structures that limit personal liability for business debts and legal actions.

- Estate Planning: Creating a comprehensive estate plan to ensure the orderly transfer of assets to heirs and minimize estate taxes.

Tax Efficiency

Tax Planning

Effective tax planning is essential for protecting wealth from excessive taxation and maximizing after-tax returns.

- Tax-Advantaged Accounts: Utilizing accounts such as IRAs, 401(k)s, and HSAs to benefit from tax deferral or tax-free growth.

- Tax-Efficient Investments: Selecting investments that generate favorable tax treatment, such as municipal bonds and index funds.

- Tax-Loss Harvesting: Selling losing investments to offset gains and reduce taxable income.

International Tax Considerations

For individuals with international assets or income, understanding and managing cross-border tax implications is crucial.

- Double Taxation Agreements: Leveraging treaties between countries to avoid double taxation on the same income.

- Offshore Accounts: Utilizing offshore accounts and trusts to benefit from favorable tax regimes, while ensuring compliance with international tax laws.

Estate Planning

Wills and Trusts

Creating wills and trusts is essential for ensuring the orderly transfer of wealth and protecting assets for future generations.

- Wills: Legal documents that outline the distribution of assets upon death, ensuring that wishes are honored.

- Trusts: Establishing trusts to manage and distribute assets according to specific terms, providing privacy, tax benefits, and protection from creditors.

Gifting Strategies

Implementing gifting strategies can reduce estate taxes and transfer wealth efficiently.

- Annual Exclusion Gifts: Taking advantage of the annual gift tax exclusion to transfer assets tax-free.

- Charitable Giving: Donating to charities for tax benefits and to support philanthropic goals.

Business Succession Planning

For business owners, creating a succession plan ensures the smooth transfer of business interests and protects the value of the business.

- Buy-Sell Agreements: Legal agreements that outline the transfer of business ownership in the event of death, disability, or retirement.

- Leadership Development: Preparing and training successors to ensure the continued success and stability of the business.

Safeguarding Digital Assets

Cybersecurity

Protecting digital assets and personal information from cyber threats is increasingly important in the digital age.

- Strong Passwords: Using complex passwords and two-factor authentication to secure online accounts.

- Encryption: Encrypting sensitive data to protect it from unauthorized access.

- Regular Updates: Keeping software and systems up to date to defend against vulnerabilities and cyber attacks.

Digital Estate Planning

Including digital assets in estate planning ensures that they are properly managed and transferred.

- Inventory of Digital Assets: Creating a comprehensive list of digital assets, such as online accounts, cryptocurrencies, and intellectual property.

- Access and Instructions: Providing instructions for accessing and managing digital assets, including passwords and security measures.

Continuous Monitoring and Review

Regular Reviews

Regularly reviewing financial plans, investments, and protection strategies is essential for adapting to changing circumstances and maintaining effective wealth protection.

- Annual Reviews: Conducting annual reviews to assess progress, update goals, and make necessary adjustments.

- Life Events: Revisiting plans following significant life events, such as marriage, divorce, the birth of a child, or retirement.

Professional Advice

Seeking advice from financial professionals ensures that wealth protection strategies are comprehensive and effective.

- Financial Advisors: Working with financial advisors to develop and implement tailored wealth protection plans.

- Legal Experts: Consult with attorneys to establish appropriate legal structures and ensure compliance with laws and regulations.

- Tax Professionals: Engaging tax professionals to optimize tax strategies and ensure adherence to tax laws.

Behavioral Aspects of Wealth Protection

Discipline and Prudence

Maintaining discipline and prudence in financial decisions is critical for protecting wealth.

- Avoiding Impulsive Decisions: Making thoughtful and informed financial decisions, rather than acting on impulse or emotion.

- Long-Term Perspective: Focusing on long-term goals and strategies, rather than short-term gains or losses.

Education and Awareness

Continuous education and awareness of financial matters enhance the ability to protect and grow wealth.

- Staying Informed: Keeping up with financial news, market trends, and changes in laws and regulations.

- Lifelong Learning: Engaging in ongoing financial education through courses, seminars, and reading.

Conclusion

The science of wealth protection involves a comprehensive approach to managing risks, utilizing insurance and legal structures, and implementing tax-efficient strategies. By understanding and applying these principles, individuals and businesses can safeguard their assets and ensure long-term financial security. Continuous monitoring, professional advice, and disciplined financial behavior are essential components of effective wealth protection. As financial landscapes evolve, staying informed and adaptable will be key to maintaining and protecting wealth for the future.

CHAPTER 10

THE SCIENCE OF MONEY AND HAPPINESS

The relationship between money and happiness is a complex and multifaceted topic that has intrigued researchers, economists, and psychologists for decades. Understanding how financial resources impact well-being involves examining the psychological, social, and economic dimensions of happiness. This chapter explores the science behind money and happiness, the factors that influence this relationship, and practical strategies for using money to enhance well-being.

Theoretical Foundations

The Economics of Happiness

The economics of happiness studies how economic factors, such as income, wealth, and consumption, influence individual and societal well-being.

- Utility Theory: In economics, utility refers to the satisfaction or happiness derived from consuming goods and services. Higher-income allows for greater consumption, potentially leading to higher utility.

- Diminishing Marginal Utility: The principle that the additional satisfaction gained from consuming one more unit of a good or service decreases as consumption increases. This implies that beyond a certain point, additional income has a diminishing impact on happiness.

Psychological Perspectives

Psychological research provides insights into how money influences happiness through various mechanisms.

- Maslow's Hierarchy of Needs: Maslow's theory suggests that basic needs (such as food, shelter, and safety) must be met before individuals can pursue higher-level needs, such as self-actualization. Money plays a crucial role in fulfilling these basic needs.

- Self-Determination Theory: This theory posits that well-being is achieved when individuals fulfill their needs for autonomy, competence, and relatedness. Money can facilitate these needs by providing resources and opportunities.

Factors Influencing the Relationship Between Money and Happiness

Income and Happiness

Research indicates a positive correlation between income and happiness, particularly at lower income levels.

- Basic Needs Fulfillment: Higher income allows individuals to meet their basic needs, reducing stress and increasing overall well-being.

- Income Threshold: Studies suggest that beyond a certain income threshold, the additional increase in happiness diminishes. This threshold varies by country and individual circumstances.

Wealth and Financial Security

Wealth and financial security contribute to happiness by providing stability and reducing anxiety about future uncertainties.

- Emergency Savings: Having a financial cushion for emergencies enhances feelings of security and reduces stress.

- Debt Management: Avoiding excessive debt and managing existing debt responsibly improves financial well-being and happiness.

Spending Patterns

How individuals spend their money can significantly impact their happiness.

- Experiential Purchases: Spending money on experiences, such as travel, dining out, and cultural activities, tends to bring more happiness than material purchases. Experiences provide lasting memories and opportunities for social connection.

- Material Purchases: While material goods can provide temporary satisfaction, they often lead to habituation and do not contribute to long-term happiness.

Social Comparisons

Social comparisons influence how individuals perceive their financial situation and overall happiness.

- Relative Income: People often compare their income and wealth to those of others. Feeling relatively poorer than peers can reduce happiness, even if absolute income is sufficient.

- Keeping Up with the Joneses: The desire to match the spending patterns of others can lead to financial strain and decreased well-being.

Practical Strategies for Using Money to Enhance Happiness

Prioritize Experiences Over Material Goods

Investing in experiences rather than material possessions can lead to greater and more lasting happiness.

- Shared Experiences: Engaging in activities with family and friends strengthens social bonds and enhances well-being.

- Personal Growth: Pursuing experiences that promote personal growth, such as learning new skills or exploring new places, contributes to long-term satisfaction.

Foster Financial Security

Building financial security is essential for reducing stress and enhancing happiness.

- Emergency Fund: Establishing an emergency fund to cover unexpected expenses provides peace of mind and financial stability.

- Debt Reduction: Prioritizing debt repayment, especially high-interest debt, improves financial well-being and reduces anxiety.

Practice Mindful Spending

Being mindful of spending habits and aligning them with personal values can increase happiness.

- Value-Based Spending: Identifying and prioritizing spending on what truly matters to you enhances satisfaction. This might include spending on hobbies, health, or charitable contributions.

- Avoid Impulse Purchases: Delaying purchases and considering their long-term value helps prevent impulsive spending and buyer's remorse.

Give to Others

Generosity and altruism are strongly linked to happiness.

- Charitable Giving: Donating to causes you care about can provide a sense of purpose and fulfillment.

- Helping Others: Spending money to help family and friends or supporting community projects enhances social connections and well-being.

Invest in Relationships

Strong social connections are a key determinant of happiness.

- Social Activities: Investing in activities that promote social interaction, such as hosting gatherings or participating in group events, strengthens relationships and increases happiness.

- Quality Time: Prioritizing spending time with loved ones over material pursuits fosters deeper connections and emotional well-being.

Cultural and Societal Influences

Cultural Differences

Cultural values and norms influence how money affects happiness.

- Collectivist vs. Individualist Cultures: In collectivist cultures, social harmony and family support are prioritized, and financial resources are often shared. In individualist cultures, personal achievement and autonomy are more emphasized.

- Cultural Attitudes Toward Wealth: Cultural attitudes toward wealth and success can shape how individuals perceive their financial situation and its impact on happiness.

Societal Structures

Societal structures, such as social safety nets and economic inequality, affect the relationship between money and happiness.

- Social Safety Nets: Robust social safety nets, including healthcare, education, and social security, provide financial security and reduce anxiety about future uncertainties.

- Economic Inequality: High levels of economic inequality can lead to social tensions and reduce overall well-being, even for those with higher incomes.

Longitudinal Perspectives

Changes Over Time

The relationship between money and happiness can change over time due to shifts in personal circumstances, societal trends, and economic conditions.

- Life Stages: Different life stages have varying financial priorities and sources of happiness. For example, younger individuals may prioritize education and career development, while older individuals may focus on retirement planning and health.

- Economic Conditions: Economic conditions, such as recessions or periods of growth, influence financial stability and perceived well-being.

Conclusion

The science of money and happiness reveals that while money can contribute to well-being, its impact is influenced by various factors, including income levels, spending patterns, social comparisons, and cultural contexts. Prioritizing experiences, fostering financial security, practicing mindful spending, giving to others, and investing in relationships are practical strategies for using money to enhance happiness. Understanding these dynamics allows individuals to make informed financial decisions that align with their values and contribute to a fulfilling and happy life. As societal and economic conditions continue to evolve, staying adaptable and focused on what truly matters will be key to maintaining a balanced and happy relationship with money.

CHAPTER 11

THE SCIENCE OF ECONOMICS

Economics is the social science that studies how individuals, businesses, governments, and societies make choices about allocating scarce resources to satisfy unlimited wants and needs. Understanding the science of economics involves examining principles, theories, and models that explain how economies function and how economic agents interact. This chapter explores the foundational concepts of economics, the different branches, key economic indicators, and the application of economic principles to real-world issues.

Fundamental Concepts in Economics

Scarcity and Choice

Scarcity refers to the fundamental economic problem of having limited resources to meet unlimited wants. This necessitates making choices about how to allocate resources efficiently.

- Opportunity Cost: The cost of forgoing the next best alternative when making a decision. It represents the benefits that could have been obtained by choosing a different option.

- Trade-offs: The compromises that individuals, businesses, and governments must make when allocating resources. Understanding trade-offs helps in making informed decisions.

Supply and Demand

The principles of supply and demand describe how prices and quantities of goods and services are determined in a market economy.

- Law of Demand: As the price of a good or service decreases, the quantity demanded increases, and vice versa, ceteris paribus (all other things being equal).

- Law of Supply: As the price of a good or service increases, the quantity supplied increases, and vice versa, ceteris paribus.

- Market Equilibrium: The point at which the quantity demanded equals the quantity supplied, resulting in a stable market price.

Marginal Analysis

Marginal analysis examines the additional benefits and costs of a decision. It is used to determine the optimal level of an economic activity.

- Marginal Benefit: The additional benefit gained from consuming or producing one more unit of a good or service.

- Marginal Cost: The additional cost incurred from consuming or producing one more unit of a good or service.

- Optimal Decision: The point at which marginal benefit equals marginal cost, maximizing net benefit.

Branches of Economics

Microeconomics

Microeconomics focuses on the behavior of individual economic agents, such as households, firms, and markets.

- Consumer Behavior: Analyzes how consumers make choices based on preferences, budget constraints, and utility maximization.

- Production and Costs: Examines how firms make production decisions, including cost structures, profit maximization, and efficiency.

- Market Structures: Studies different market environments, such as perfect competition, monopolistic competition, oligopoly, and monopoly, and their impact on prices and output.

Macroeconomics

Macroeconomics examines the economy as a whole, focusing on aggregate variables and economic policies.

- Gross Domestic Product (GDP): Measures the total value of goods and services produced within a country's borders in a specific time period.

- Unemployment: Analyzes the level of joblessness in an economy and its causes, such as cyclical, structural, and frictional unemployment.

- Inflation: Studies the overall increase in prices and the purchasing power of money. Inflation is measured by indices like the Consumer Price Index (CPI) and Producer Price Index (PPI).

- Monetary and Fiscal Policy: Explores the tools and effects of government policies on the economy, including interest rates, money supply, taxation, and government spending.

Key Economic Indicators

Gross Domestic Product (GDP)

GDP is the primary indicator of a country's economic performance and measures the total value of goods and services produced over a specific period.

- Real GDP: Adjusted for inflation, providing a more accurate reflection of an economy's size and growth rate.

- Nominal GDP: Measured at current prices, without adjusting for inflation.

- GDP Per Capita: GDP divided by the population, indicating the average economic output per person.

Unemployment Rate

The unemployment rate measures the percentage of the labor force that is unemployed and actively seeking work.

- Cyclical Unemployment: Results from economic downturns and fluctuates with the business cycle.

- Structural Unemployment: Arises from changes in the economy, such as technological advancements or shifts in consumer demand, that make certain skills obsolete.

- Frictional Unemployment: Occurs as workers transition between jobs or enter the labor force for the first time.

Inflation Rate

The inflation rate measures the rate at which the general level of prices for goods and services is rising.

- Consumer Price Index (CPI): Tracks changes in the price level of a basket of consumer goods and services over time.

- Producer Price Index (PPI): Measures changes in the prices received by domestic producers for their output.

Economic Theories and Models

Classical Economics

Classical economics, developed in the 18th and 19th centuries, emphasizes the role of free markets and the idea that economies are self-regulating.

- Invisible Hand: Adam Smith's concept that individuals pursuing their self-interest inadvertently contribute to the overall economic well-being.

- Laissez-Faire: The belief that minimal government intervention leads to more efficient economic outcomes.

Keynesian Economics

Keynesian economics, developed by John Maynard Keynes in the 20th century, focuses on total spending in the economy and its effects on output and inflation.

- Aggregate Demand: The total demand for goods and services in an economy. Keynesians believe that insufficient aggregate demand leads to unemployment and economic downturns.

- Fiscal Policy: The use of government spending and taxation to influence economic activity and stabilize the economy.

Supply-Side Economics

Supply-side economics emphasizes the importance of production and supply factors in driving economic growth.

- Tax Cuts: Advocates for reducing taxes on businesses and individuals to encourage investment, production, and economic growth.

- Regulation Reduction: Promotes the removal of government regulations that hinder business activities and innovation.

Application of Economic Principles

Economic Policy

Economic policies are used to manage and stabilize economies, promote growth, and address issues like unemployment and inflation.

- Monetary Policy: Central banks use tools such as interest rates, open market operations, and reserve requirements to control the money supply and influence economic activity.

- Fiscal Policy: Governments adjust spending and taxation to manage economic performance, influence aggregate demand, and achieve social goals.

International Trade

International trade involves the exchange of goods and services between countries, driven by the principle of comparative advantage.

- Comparative Advantage: The ability of a country to produce a good or service at a lower opportunity cost than others, leading to more efficient global production and trade.

- Trade Policies: Governments use tariffs, quotas, and trade agreements to regulate international trade and protect domestic industries.

Behavioral Economics

Behavioral economics combines insights from psychology and economics to understand how individuals make economic decisions.

- Bounded Rationality: The idea that individuals make decisions based on limited information and cognitive constraints.

- Nudge Theory: Proposes subtle interventions to encourage better decision-making without restricting freedom of choice.

Economic Challenges and Future Directions

Globalization

Globalization has increased economic interdependence among countries, leading to both opportunities and challenges.

- Economic Integration: Greater integration of global markets can lead to increased trade, investment, and economic growth.

- Income Inequality: Globalization can exacerbate income inequality within and between countries, requiring policies to address disparities.

Technological Advancements

Technological advancements are transforming economies and labor markets.

- Automation and AI: Automation and artificial intelligence can enhance productivity but also displace jobs, necessitating workforce retraining and education.

- Digital Economy: The rise of the digital economy creates new opportunities for innovation and growth, while also presenting regulatory and privacy challenges.

Environmental Sustainability

Balancing economic growth with environmental sustainability is a critical challenge for the future.

- Sustainable Development: Promotes economic growth that meets the needs of the present without compromising the ability of future generations to meet their own needs.

- Green Economy: Emphasizes the importance of environmentally sustainable economic activities and the transition to renewable energy sources.

Conclusion

The science of economics provides a framework for understanding how individuals, businesses, governments, and societies make choices about allocating scarce resources. By examining fundamental concepts, branches of economics, key economic indicators, and real-world applications, we gain insights into the functioning of economies and the factors that influence economic well-being. As global challenges and opportunities evolve, the principles and theories of economics will continue to guide decision-making and policy development, shaping the future of economies worldwide.

CHAPTER 12

THE GOLD STANDARD AND FIAT CURRENCY

The Gold Standard: A Historical Perspective

Origins of the Gold Standard

The gold standard is a monetary system where a country's currency or paper money has a value directly linked to gold. Countries adhered to this standard by ensuring that their currency could be exchanged for a specific amount of gold.

- Early Use of Gold: Gold has been used as a form of money for thousands of years due to its intrinsic value, durability, and divisibility. Ancient civilizations, such as the Egyptians, Greeks, and Romans, utilized gold in trade and as a measure of wealth.

- Formal Adoption: The formal adoption of the gold standard began in the 19th century. The United Kingdom was the first to adopt it officially in 1821, setting a precedent for other nations.

Mechanisms of the Gold Standard

Under the gold standard, the value of a country's currency is directly tied to a specific amount of gold. This system required countries to maintain large gold reserves to back their currency. The primary mechanisms included:

- Fixed Exchange Rates: Currencies were valued in terms of a fixed quantity of gold, establishing a stable exchange rate between countries.

- Gold Convertibility: Citizens and foreign governments could exchange currency for gold at the established rate.

- Gold Reserves: Central banks and governments maintained gold reserves to support the currency's value and ensure convertibility.

Benefits of the Gold Standard

1. Price Stability: The gold standard provided long-term price stability by limiting the ability of governments to print money excessively.

2. International Trade: Fixed exchange rates facilitated international trade and investment by reducing exchange rate risk.

3. Trust and Confidence: The gold standard promoted trust in the currency, as its value was backed by a tangible asset.

Challenges and Limitations

1. Limited Flexibility: The gold standard restricted governments' ability to respond to economic crises by adjusting monetary policy.

2. Deflationary Pressures: The limited supply of gold could lead to deflation, harming economic growth and employment.

3. Dependency on Gold Supply: Economic stability depended on the discovery and availability of new gold supplies, which were uncertain and irregular.

Transition to Fiat Currency

Decline of the Gold Standard

The gold standard began to decline during the early 20th century due to its inherent limitations and the economic challenges of the time.

- World War I: The war disrupted international trade and led many countries to suspend gold convertibility to finance military expenditures.

- Great Depression: The global economic crisis of the 1930s highlighted the rigidity of the gold standard, prompting countries to abandon it in favor of more flexible monetary policies.

Bretton Woods System

After World War II, the Bretton Woods Conference in 1944 established a new international monetary system. The US dollar was pegged to gold, and other currencies were pegged to the dollar, creating a modified gold standard.

- Dollar Convertibility: The US promised to convert dollars into gold at a fixed rate of $35 per ounce, ensuring stability.

- Fixed Exchange Rates: Countries maintained fixed exchange rates to the dollar, promoting international economic stability and growth.

End of the Bretton Woods System

The Bretton Woods system began to unravel in the 1960s due to persistent balance-of-payments deficits and the inability of the US to maintain the dollar's gold convertibility.

- Nixon Shock: In 1971, President Richard Nixon suspended the convertibility of the dollar into gold, effectively ending the Bretton Woods system.

- Floating Exchange Rates: By 1973, most major currencies had shifted to floating exchange rates, marking the transition to a fiat currency system.

The Fiat Currency System

Definition of Fiat Currency

Fiat currency is money that has no intrinsic value and is not backed by a physical commodity like gold. Instead, its value is derived from the trust and confidence of the people who use it.

- Government Decree: Fiat currency is established and regulated by government decree, making it legal tender for all debts, public and private.

- Unlimited Supply: Governments can issue fiat currency in any amount, providing greater flexibility in monetary policy.

Advantages of Fiat Currency

1. Monetary Flexibility: Central banks can adjust the money supply and interest rates to manage economic cycles, combat inflation, and stimulate growth.

2. Economic Stability: Fiat currency allows for more responsive fiscal and monetary policies, helping to stabilize economies during crises.

3. Reduced Dependency on Gold: Economies are no longer constrained by the availability of gold, allowing for greater economic expansion.

Challenges of Fiat Currency

1. Inflation Risk: Without the discipline of the gold standard, there is a risk of excessive money printing, leading to inflation or hyperinflation.

2. Trust and Confidence: The value of fiat currency relies on public trust in the issuing government and its monetary policies. Mismanagement can erode this trust.

3. Debt and Deficits: Fiat currency systems can enable governments to accumulate high levels of debt, which may pose long-term economic risks.

Implications for Monetary Systems

The transition from the gold standard to fiat currency has profound implications for modern monetary systems:

- Central Bank Independence: Central banks play a crucial role in managing fiat currency, requiring independence from political pressures to maintain credibility and effectiveness.

- Global Financial System: The fiat currency system underpins the global financial system, with floating exchange rates and international capital flows shaping economic interactions.

- Economic Policy: Fiat currency provides the tools for more nuanced and effective economic policy, allowing for targeted interventions to address specific economic issues.

Conclusion

The gold standard and fiat currency represent two distinct approaches to managing money and economic stability. While the gold standard provided long-term price stability and trust, its rigidity and dependence on gold supply limited its effectiveness in a dynamic global economy. The transition to fiat currency has brought greater flexibility and adaptability, allowing for more responsive monetary policy and economic management. Understanding this evolution is crucial for appreciating the complexities of modern monetary systems and the ongoing challenges they face.

CHAPTER 13

CENTRAL BANKING AND MONETARY POLICY

The Role of Central Banks

Central banks are pivotal institutions in the economic and financial systems of countries. Their primary mandate is to ensure economic stability through the management of monetary policy, regulation of the banking sector, and maintenance of financial stability.

Functions of Central Banks

1. Monetary Policy Implementation: Central banks control the money supply and interest rates to achieve macroeconomic objectives such as controlling inflation, managing employment levels, and promoting economic growth.

2. Financial Supervision and Regulation: They oversee the banking and financial systems to ensure stability, protect depositors, and prevent systemic risks.

3. Currency Issuance: Central banks have the sole authority to issue national currency, ensuring an adequate and stable money supply.

4. Government's Banker: Central banks manage the government's accounts, facilitate payments, and handle the issuance of government bonds.

5. Lender of Last Resort: In times of financial crisis, central banks provide liquidity to banks facing short-term solvency issues to maintain confidence and prevent bank runs.

Tools of Monetary Policy

Central banks have a variety of tools at their disposal to influence the money supply and economic conditions.

Open Market Operations (OMO)

Open market operations are the most commonly used tool of monetary policy. Central banks buy and sell government securities in the open market to regulate the money supply and influence short-term interest rates.

- Expansionary OMO: When the central bank buys government securities, it injects liquidity into the banking system, lowering interest rates and encouraging borrowing and investment.

- Contractionary OMO: Selling government securities withdraws liquidity from the banking system, raising interest rates and curbing borrowing and spending.

Interest Rates

Central banks set benchmark interest rates, such as the federal funds rate in the United States, which influence the cost of borrowing and the level of economic activity.

- Lowering Interest Rates: Reduces the cost of borrowing, stimulates consumer spending and business investment, and can boost economic growth.

- Raising Interest Rates: Increases the cost of borrowing, discourages spending and investment, and helps to control inflation.

Reserve Requirements

Reserve requirements refer to the minimum amount of reserves that banks must hold against their deposits. By changing these requirements, central banks can influence the money supply.

- Lowering Reserve Requirements: Frees up more funds for banks to lend, increasing the money supply and stimulating economic activity.

- Raising Reserve Requirements: Restricts the amount of money banks can lend, reducing the money supply and curbing inflation.

Quantitative Easing (QE)

Quantitative easing is a non-traditional monetary policy tool used during times of economic crisis when standard tools are insufficient. It involves the central bank purchasing long-term securities, such as government bonds and mortgage-backed securities, to inject liquidity directly into the economy.

- Purpose of QE: Lower long-term interest rates, increase asset prices, and encourage lending and investment.

- Risks of QE: Potential for creating asset bubbles and long-term inflationary pressures.

Impact of Monetary Policy on Economic Stability

Monetary policy plays a crucial role in maintaining economic stability, influencing various aspects of the economy.

Inflation Control

One of the primary objectives of monetary policy is to control inflation. Central banks aim to keep inflation within a target range, typically around 2%, to ensure price stability.

- Inflation Targeting: Central banks use interest rates and other tools to manage inflation expectations and keep actual inflation close to the target.

- Hyperinflation and Deflation: Effective monetary policy helps prevent extreme scenarios such as hyperinflation (excessive price increases) and deflation (a persistent decline in prices).

Economic Growth and Employment

Monetary policy also aims to promote sustainable economic growth and high levels of employment.

- Stimulative Policies: Lowering interest rates and increasing the money supply can boost economic activity, reduce unemployment, and support growth.

- Contractionary Policies: Raising interest rates and tightening the money supply can slow down an overheating economy, preventing unsustainable booms and subsequent busts.

Financial Stability

Central banks play a critical role in maintaining the stability of the financial system.

- Crisis Management: During financial crises, central banks act as lenders of last resort, providing liquidity to troubled banks and preventing systemic collapse.

\- Macroprudential Regulation: Central banks implement regulations to monitor and mitigate systemic risks, ensuring the resilience of the financial system.

Case Studies in Monetary Policy

The Federal Reserve and the Great Recession

During the Great Recession of 2007-2009, the Federal Reserve implemented several unprecedented monetary policy measures to stabilize the economy.

\- Interest Rate Cuts: The Fed lowered the federal funds rate to near zero to stimulate borrowing and spending.

\- Quantitative Easing: Multiple rounds of QE involved purchasing large quantities of government and mortgage-backed securities to inject liquidity into the economy.

\- Outcome: These measures helped stabilize financial markets, support economic recovery, and prevent a deeper recession.

The European Central Bank (ECB) and the Eurozone Crisis

The Eurozone crisis in the early 2010s posed significant challenges for the ECB.

\- Interest Rate Reductions: The ECB lowered interest rates to historic lows to stimulate economic activity.

- Long-Term Refinancing Operations (LTRO): Provided cheap long-term loans to banks to ensure liquidity and support lending.

- Outright Monetary Transactions (OMT): The ECB announced it would buy government bonds of struggling Eurozone countries to stabilize their economies.

- Outcome: These measures helped restore confidence, stabilize financial markets, and support economic recovery in the Eurozone.

Conclusion

Central banks are vital institutions that play a key role in ensuring economic stability through the implementation of monetary policy. By using tools such as open market operations, interest rates, reserve requirements, and quantitative easing, central banks influence the money supply, control inflation, and support economic growth and financial stability. Understanding the role and impact of central banks is essential for comprehending the complexities of modern economic systems and the policies that shape our economic landscape. As economic conditions evolve, central banks will continue to adapt their strategies to meet new challenges and maintain stability in the global economy.

CHAPTER 14

DIGITAL CURRENCIES AND CRYPTOCURRENCIES

The Rise of Digital Currencies

Digital currencies have transformed the financial landscape, offering new ways to transact, save, and invest. They encompass both centralized digital currencies, issued and regulated by governments or financial institutions, and decentralized cryptocurrencies, which operate independently of central authorities.

Definition and Types of Digital Currencies

- Digital Currency: A form of money that exists only in digital form and is not tangible like paper money or coins. It includes both cryptocurrencies and digital versions of fiat currencies.

- Cryptocurrency: A type of digital currency that uses cryptographic techniques for security, operating on decentralized networks based on blockchain technology.

Blockchain Technology

What is Blockchain?

Blockchain is the underlying technology behind most cryptocurrencies. It is a distributed ledger that records all transactions across a network of computers.

- Decentralized: No central authority controls the blockchain; instead, it is maintained by a network of nodes (computers) that validate and record transactions.

- Immutable: Once recorded, transactions cannot be altered or deleted, ensuring transparency and security.

- Consensus Mechanisms: Methods like Proof of Work (PoW) or Proof of Stake (PoS) ensure that all participants agree on the validity of transactions.

How Blockchain Works

1. Transaction Initiation: A user initiates a transaction, which is then broadcast to the network.

2. Validation: Network nodes validate the transaction using cryptographic algorithms.

3. Block Formation: Validated transactions are grouped into a block.

4. Consensus: The network reaches a consensus on the block's validity.

5. Addition to Blockchain: The block is added to the existing blockchain, making the transaction permanent.

6. Completion: The transaction is complete and visible to all participants in the network.

Major Cryptocurrencies

Bitcoin (BTC)

- Introduction: Launched in 2009 by an anonymous entity known as Satoshi Nakamoto.

- Significance: The first and most widely recognized cryptocurrency.

- Technology: Uses Proof of Work (PoW) for consensus.

- Supply Limit: Capped at 21 million coins.

Ethereum (ETH)

- Introduction: Created by Vitalik Buterin and launched in 2015.

- Significance: Known for its smart contract functionality, enabling decentralized applications (dApps).

- Technology: Transitioning from Proof of Work (PoW) to Proof of Stake (PoS) with Ethereum 2.0.

- Supply: No fixed cap, with annual issuance reducing over time.

Other Notable Cryptocurrencies

- Ripple (XRP): Focuses on facilitating real-time cross-border payments for financial institutions.

- Litecoin (LTC): Created as a "lighter" version of Bitcoin with faster transaction times and a different hashing algorithm.

- Cardano (ADA): Emphasizes a research-driven approach to blockchain development and sustainability.

Benefits of Cryptocurrencies

Decentralization

Cryptocurrencies operate on decentralized networks, reducing the need for intermediaries like banks and allowing for peer-to-peer transactions.

- Lower Fees: Reduced reliance on intermediaries can lead to lower transaction fees.

- Increased Security: Decentralization reduces the risk of single points of failure and cyber attacks.

Financial Inclusion

Cryptocurrencies can provide financial services to unbanked and underbanked populations, especially in regions with limited access to traditional banking.

- Accessibility: Anyone with an internet connection can participate in the cryptocurrency economy.

- Lower Barriers: Reduced requirements for opening accounts and conducting transactions.

Transparency and Security

Blockchain technology ensures transparency and security through immutable transaction records and cryptographic validation.

- Transparency: All transactions are publicly visible on the blockchain, promoting accountability.

- Security: Cryptographic techniques and decentralized validation protect against fraud and tampering.

Challenges Posed by Cryptocurrencies

Regulatory Concerns

Cryptocurrencies operate in a legal gray area in many jurisdictions, leading to uncertainty and potential regulatory challenges.

- Regulation: Governments are grappling with how to regulate cryptocurrencies without stifling innovation.

- Compliance: Cryptocurrencies must navigate a complex web of anti-money laundering (AML) and know-your-customer (KYC) regulations.

Volatility

Cryptocurrencies are known for their price volatility, which can pose risks for investors and users.

- Price Swings: Significant fluctuations in value can impact the stability of the cryptocurrency market.

- Investor Risk: High volatility can lead to substantial financial losses for investors.

Security and Fraud

While blockchain itself is secure, the broader cryptocurrency ecosystem faces security challenges.

- Exchanges: Cryptocurrency exchanges have been targets for hacking and fraud.

- Scams: The anonymity of cryptocurrencies can facilitate scams and illicit activities.

The Future of Digital Currencies

Central Bank Digital Currencies (CBDCs)

Many central banks are exploring or piloting digital versions of their national currencies.

- Advantages: CBDCs can combine the efficiency of digital currencies with the stability of fiat money.

- Implementation: Examples include China's digital yuan and ongoing research by the European Central Bank.

Integration with Traditional Financial Systems

Cryptocurrencies and digital currencies are increasingly being integrated into traditional financial systems.

- Adoption: Financial institutions are starting to offer cryptocurrency services, including trading and custody.

- Innovation: Blockchain technology is being leveraged for various financial applications, such as supply chain finance and cross-border payments.

Conclusion

Digital currencies and cryptocurrencies represent a significant evolution in the world of finance. Their rise, driven by technological advancements and a desire for greater financial inclusion and efficiency, poses both opportunities and challenges for traditional monetary systems. As the landscape continues to evolve, the interplay between digital currencies, regulatory frameworks, and traditional financial institutions will shape the future of money and finance. Understanding these dynamics is crucial for navigating the complexities of this rapidly changing field.

CHAPTER 15

INTERNATIONAL MONETARY SYSTEMS

Introduction to International Monetary Systems

International monetary systems govern the rules and conventions for financial interactions between countries, facilitating trade, investment, and economic stability on a global scale. This chapter delves into the dynamics of global currencies, exchange rates, and the various international monetary arrangements that have shaped the global economy.

Dynamics of Global Currencies

Major Global Currencies

Global currencies are those widely used in international trade and finance. The most prominent include:

- US Dollar (USD): The primary global reserve currency, used in most international transactions.

- Euro (EUR): The currency of the Eurozone, the second most traded currency globally.

- Japanese Yen (JPY): A major currency in Asia and the third most traded currency.

- British Pound (GBP): Historically significant, still a key currency in global finance.

- Chinese Yuan (CNY): Increasingly influential, reflecting China's growing economic power.

Factors Influencing Currency Value

The value of a currency in the foreign exchange market is influenced by various factors, including:

- Economic Indicators: GDP growth, employment rates, inflation, and interest rates.

- Political Stability: Countries with stable governments tend to have stronger currencies.

- Market Sentiment: Investor perceptions and speculative activities can affect currency value.

- Trade Balances: A surplus (exports > imports) tends to strengthen a currency, while a deficit weakens it.

- Monetary Policy: Central bank actions, such as interest rate changes and quantitative easing, impact currency value.

Exchange Rates

Types of Exchange Rate Systems

1. Fixed Exchange Rate: A country pegs its currency's value to another currency or a basket of currencies. Central banks maintain the fixed rate by buying and selling their currency.

2. Floating Exchange Rate: Currency values fluctuate based on market forces without direct government or central bank intervention.

3. Managed Float: Also known as a "dirty float," where exchange rates primarily fluctuate based on market forces, but central banks occasionally intervene to stabilize or influence the currency.

Determinants of Exchange Rates

- Supply and Demand: Exchange rates are determined by the supply and demand for different currencies in the foreign exchange market.

- Interest Rate Differentials: Higher interest rates offer lenders a better return relative to other countries, attracting foreign capital and causing the currency to appreciate.

- Inflation Rates: Lower inflation in a country relative to others will increase its currency value as purchasing power is maintained.

- Economic Performance: Strong economic performance attracts investment and increases demand for the currency.

Historical and Modern International Monetary Arrangements

The Bretton Woods System

Established in 1944, the Bretton Woods system aimed to create a stable international monetary framework post-World War II.

- Fixd Exchange Rates: Currencies were pegged to the US dollar, which was convertible to gold at $35 per ounce.

- International Monetary Fund (IMF): Created to oversee the international monetary system, provide financial assistance to countries facing balance of payments issues, and ensure stability.

- World Bank: Established to provide financial and technical assistance for reconstruction and development.

Collapse of Bretton Woods

The Bretton Woods system collapsed in the early 1970s due to several factors:

- US Dollar Pressure: Increasing US trade deficits and spending led to doubts about the dollar's ability to maintain its gold convertibility.

- Nixon Shock: In 1971, President Richard Nixon suspended the dollar's convertibility into gold, leading to the system's collapse and the transition to floating exchange rates by 1973.

Post-Bretton Woods Era

The post-Bretton Woods era is characterized by floating exchange rates and increased financial globalization.

- Flexible Exchange Rates: Most major currencies now float freely, determined by market forces.

- Increased Volatility: Floating rates can lead to more exchange rate volatility, affecting international trade and investment.

- IMF Role: The IMF continues to play a crucial role in monitoring global financial stability, providing financial assistance, and advising on policy.

The Role of the International Monetary Fund (IMF)

IMF Objectives

- Financial Stability: Promotes international monetary cooperation and exchange rate stability.

- Economic Growth: Facilitates balanced growth of international trade.

- Assistance Programs: Provides resources to member countries facing balance of payments problems.

IMF Tools and Functions

- Surveillance: Monitors global economic trends and assesses financial vulnerabilities.

- Financial Assistance: Provides loans to member countries with balance of payments issues, often with conditionality to implement economic reforms.

- Technical Assistance: Offers expertise and training to member countries to strengthen their economic institutions and policies.

Modern International Monetary Issues

Global Financial Integration

The integration of global financial markets has increased the interdependence of economies.

- Capital Flows: Increased cross-border capital flows can enhance growth but also lead to financial contagion.

- Regulatory Challenges: Coordination of financial regulations to manage risks and ensure stability is a continuous challenge.

Currency Wars and Exchange Rate Manipulation

Some countries may engage in competitive devaluation to gain a trade advantage, leading to "currency wars."

- Impact on Trade: Currency manipulation can distort trade balances and create tensions between countries.

- International Response: Organizations like the IMF monitor and address unfair exchange rate practices.

Conclusion

The dynamics of international monetary systems are complex and ever-evolving. The transition from fixed exchange rates under the Bretton Woods system to the current regime of floating rates has significantly altered the global financial landscape. Central to this system is the role of the IMF, which continues to provide oversight and support to ensure stability and growth in the global economy. Understanding these systems, their history, and their functioning is crucial for comprehending the intricacies of international finance and trade. As globalization continues to deepen, the interplay between global currencies, exchange rates, and international monetary arrangements will remain a critical area of focus for policymakers and economists.

CHAPTER 16

FINANCIAL MARKETS AND MONEY MARKETS

Introduction to Financial Markets

Financial markets are platforms where buyers and sellers engage in the trade of financial assets such as stocks, bonds, currencies, and derivatives. These markets play a crucial role in the allocation of resources, the pricing of assets, and the stability and growth of the broader economy.

Functions of Financial Markets

Price Discovery

Financial markets facilitate price discovery, the process by which market prices are determined through the interaction of buyers and sellers. This process reflects the supply and demand dynamics and incorporates all available information about an asset.

Liquidity Provision

Markets provide liquidity, allowing participants to buy and sell assets quickly without causing significant price changes. High liquidity reduces transaction costs and risks, encouraging more trading activity.

Capital Allocation

Financial markets allocate capital efficiently by directing funds to their most productive uses. Companies and governments can raise capital by issuing stocks or bonds, while investors seek to invest in assets offering the best risk-adjusted returns.

Risk Management

Through various financial instruments and derivatives, markets enable participants to hedge against risks such as interest rate changes, currency fluctuations, and commodity price variations. This risk management is crucial for businesses and investors to protect their portfolios and operations.

Economic Indicator

The performance of financial markets often reflects the broader economic conditions. Rising markets typically indicate economic growth and investor confidence, while falling markets may signal economic downturns or instability.

Types of Financial Markets

Equity Markets

Equity markets, or stock markets, are platforms where shares of publicly traded companies are bought and sold. Major equity markets include the New York Stock Exchange (NYSE) and the Nasdaq.

- Primary Market: Companies issue new shares to raise capital through initial public offerings (IPOs).

- Secondary Market: Investors trade existing shares, providing liquidity and continuous price discovery.

Debt Markets

Debt markets, or bond markets, involve the issuance and trading of debt securities. These markets include government bonds, corporate bonds, and municipal bonds.

- Primary Market: Issuers sell new bonds to investors to raise funds.

- Secondary Market: Existing bonds are traded among investors, allowing for liquidity and portfolio adjustments.

Derivatives Markets

Derivatives markets deal with financial contracts whose value is derived from underlying assets such as stocks, bonds, commodities, or currencies. Common derivatives include options, futures, and swaps.

- Risk Management: Derivatives allow participants to hedge against price movements and manage financial risk.

- Speculation: Traders use derivatives to speculate on the future direction of asset prices, seeking profit from price changes.

Foreign Exchange Markets

Foreign exchange (Forex) markets facilitate the trading of currencies. They are the largest and most liquid financial markets globally, with major centers in London, New York, and Tokyo.

- Currency Pairs: Currencies are traded in pairs (e.g., EUR/USD), with the exchange rate representing the relative value of one currency to another.

- Impact on Trade: Forex markets influence international trade by affecting exchange rates, which determine the cost of imports and exports.

Commodity Markets

Commodity markets involve the trading of physical goods such as oil, gold, and agricultural products. These markets are crucial for price discovery and risk management in industries reliant on raw materials.

- Spot Market: Physical commodities are bought and sold for immediate delivery.

- Futures Market: Contracts are traded to buy or sell commodities at a future date, allowing for price hedging and speculation.

Money Markets

Definition and Role

Money markets are segments of the financial markets where short-term debt instruments with high liquidity and short maturities are traded. These instruments typically mature in less than one year and include Treasury bills, commercial paper, and certificates of deposit.

Functions of Money Markets

. Liquidity Management: Money markets provide a mechanism for managing short-term liquidity needs for financial institutions, corporations, and governments.

2. Interest Rate Benchmarking: Short-term interest rates in money markets serve as benchmarks for various financial products and services.

3. Safe Investment Avenue: Investors seek safe and liquid investment options in money markets, preserving capital while earning modest returns.

4. Efficient Allocation of Short-Term Funds: Money markets facilitate the efficient allocation of short-term funds, ensuring that surplus funds are directed to where they are needed most.

Key Instruments in Money Markets

Treasury Bills (T-Bills)

- Issuer: Government

- Maturity: Typically 4 weeks, 13 weeks, 26 weeks, or 52 weeks

- Risk: Low, considered one of the safest investments

- Purpose: Used by governments to manage short-term funding needs and by investors seeking a safe, short-term investment.

Commercial Paper

- Issuer: Corporations

- Maturity: Usually 1 to 270 days

- Risk: Higher than T-Bills, depending on the issuer's creditworthiness

- Purpose: Provides short-term funding for corporate expenses such as inventory and accounts payable.

Certificates of Deposit (CDs)

- Issuer: Banks and financial institutions

- Maturity: Can range from a few weeks to several years, though typically short-term in money markets

- Risk: Low, but higher than T-Bills, with insured deposits being the safest

- Purpose: Allows banks to attract short-term deposits and provides a higher return than regular savings accounts.

Repurchase Agreements (Repos)

\- Issuer: Typically financial institutions

\- Maturity: Overnight to a few weeks

\- Risk: Low, secured by collateral

\- Purpose: Used for short-term borrowing and lending, where one party sells securities with an agreement to repurchase them at a later date.

Impact on the Broader Economy

Economic Stability

Financial and money markets contribute to economic stability by ensuring efficient capital allocation, liquidity provision, and risk management. These markets help prevent systemic crises by providing mechanisms for managing financial risks.

Economic Growth

By facilitating investment and funding for businesses and governments, financial markets drive economic growth. They enable companies to expand, innovate, and create jobs, contributing to overall economic development.

Monetary Policy Implementation

Central banks use money markets to implement monetary policy by influencing short-term interest rates. Through open market operations, central banks can manage liquidity in the financial system, control inflation, and stabilize the economy.

Financial Inclusion

Efficient financial markets contribute to financial inclusion by providing individuals and businesses with access to capital, investment opportunities, and financial services, fostering economic participation and development.

Conclusion

Financial markets and money markets play a vital role in the global economy, influencing everything from investment and capital allocation to monetary policy and economic stability. By providing platforms for trading financial assets and managing liquidity and risk, these markets ensure the efficient functioning of the broader economy. Understanding their functions, instruments, and impact is essential for comprehending the complexities of modern financial systems and their role in promoting economic growth and stability. As financial markets continue to evolve, their significance in shaping global economic trends will remain paramount.

CHAPTER 17

FINANCIAL CRISES AND BANKING FAILURES

Introduction to Financial Crises

Financial crises are periods of severe disruptions in financial markets, characterized by sharp declines in asset prices, failures of financial institutions, and contractions in economic activity. Understanding the causes, effects, and regulatory responses to financial crises is essential for preventing future occurrences and mitigating their impact.

Historical Financial Crises

The Great Depression (1929-1939)

Causes:

- Stock Market Crash: The collapse of the US stock market in October 1929 wiped out significant wealth and confidence.

- Bank Failures: A series of bank runs led to widespread bank failures, exacerbating the economic downturn.

- Monetary Contraction: The Federal Reserve's tightening of monetary policy reduced the money supply, deepening the recession.

- Global Trade Decline: Protectionist policies, such as the Smoot-Hawley Tariff, reduced international trade and worsened global economic conditions.

Effects:

- Mass Unemployment: Unemployment rates soared to unprecedented levels.

- Deflation: Falling prices led to decreased consumer spending and business investment.

- Economic Contraction: GDP declined sharply, and industrial production plummeted.

Regulatory Responses:

- New Deal Programs: The US government implemented extensive public works programs and social safety nets.

- Banking Reforms: The Glass-Steagall Act separated commercial and investment banking, and the Federal Deposit

Insurance Corporation (FDIC) was established to protect depositors.

- Monetary Policy Changes: The Federal Reserve adopted more active and expansionary policies to stabilize the economy.

The Asian Financial Crisis (1997-1998)

Causes:

- Currency Speculation: Massive speculative attacks on Southeast Asian currencies led to sharp devaluations.

- Overleveraging: Excessive borrowing by businesses and governments, often in foreign currencies, created vulnerabilities.

- Weak Financial Systems: Poorly regulated banking sectors and inadequate risk management practices exacerbated the crisis.

Effects:

- Economic Recession: Rapid declines in GDP and soaring unemployment rates across affected countries.

- Currency Depreciation: Sharp declines in currency values led to inflation and increased debt burdens.

- Social Unrest: Economic hardship led to political instability and social unrest in several countries.

Regulatory Responses:

- International Bailouts: The International Monetary Fund (IMF) provided financial assistance to stabilize economies.

- Structural Reforms: Affected countries implemented financial sector reforms, improved regulatory frameworks, and enhanced corporate governance.

- Currency Stabilization: Countries adopted measures to stabilize their currencies and restore investor confidence.

The Global Financial Crisis (2007-2008)

Causes:

- Housing Bubble: A rapid increase in housing prices fueled by easy credit and speculative investments.

- Subprime Mortgages: High-risk lending practices led to a proliferation of subprime mortgages, which were packaged into mortgage-backed securities (MBS) and sold to investors.

- Leverage and Risk: Financial institutions engaged in excessive leverage and risk-taking, often using complex financial derivatives.

- Regulatory Failures: Inadequate oversight and regulation of financial markets and institutions allowed systemic risks to build.

Effects:

- Bank Failures: Major financial institutions, including Lehman Brothers, collapsed, leading to a loss of confidence and a credit crunch.

- Economic Recession: Global GDP contracted, unemployment rates soared, and international trade declined.

- Wealth Destruction: Significant losses in stock markets and housing values reduced household wealth and consumer spending.

Regulatory Responses:

- Emergency Measures: Governments and central banks implemented unprecedented measures, including bank bailouts, liquidity injections, and interest rate cuts.

- Regulatory Reforms: The Dodd-Frank Act in the US introduced comprehensive financial regulation, including the establishment of the Consumer Financial Protection Bureau (CFPB) and enhanced oversight of systemic risks.

- International Coordination: Global financial regulators and institutions, such as the G20 and the Financial Stability Board (FSB), coordinated efforts to reform and stabilize the financial system.

Causes of Financial Crises

Excessive Leverage

High levels of borrowing by individuals, businesses, and financial institutions increase vulnerability to economic shocks and can lead to financial instability.

Asset Bubbles

Rapid increases in asset prices, driven by speculative investment and easy credit, can create bubbles that eventually burst, leading to sharp declines in wealth and economic activity.

Regulatory Failures

Inadequate regulation and oversight of financial markets and institutions can allow systemic risks to build up, contributing to financial crises.

Macroeconomic Imbalances

Large and persistent imbalances, such as current account deficits, excessive public debt, or large capital inflows, can create vulnerabilities that precipitate financial crises.

Effects of Financial Crises on Money Systems

Banking Sector Stress

Financial crises often lead to widespread banking sector stress, including bank runs, insolvencies, and a contraction in lending. This can reduce the money supply and exacerbate economic downturns.

Currency Depreciation

Currency values can decline sharply during financial crises, leading to inflation, increased debt burdens for borrowers with foreign currency loans, and reduced purchasing power.

Fiscal Strain

Governments may face fiscal strain due to the need for emergency spending, bailouts, and economic stimulus measures, leading to increased public debt and long-term fiscal challenges.

Role of Regulatory Measures

Prudential Regulation

Strengthening prudential regulation, including capital adequacy requirements, liquidity standards, and risk management practices, can enhance the resilience of financial institutions and reduce the likelihood of crises.

Macroprudential Policies

Implementing macroprudential policies that address systemic risks, such as countercyclical capital buffers and stress testing, can help mitigate the buildup of vulnerabilities in the financial system.

Financial Supervision

Enhancing financial supervision, including the monitoring of large, interconnected financial institutions and the use of early warning systems, can improve the detection and management of risks.

Crisis Management Frameworks

Developing robust crisis management frameworks, including resolution mechanisms for failing financial institutions and coordinated international responses, can improve the effectiveness of crisis interventions.

Conclusion

Financial crises and banking failures have significant and far-reaching impacts on economies and money systems. Understanding the causes, effects, and regulatory responses to these crises is essential for building more resilient financial systems and preventing future occurrences. As financial markets continue to evolve, ongoing efforts to enhance regulation, supervision, and crisis management will be crucial for maintaining economic stability and protecting against the devastating consequences of financial crises.

.

CHAPTER 18

THE FUTURE OF MONEY

Introduction to the Future of Money

The future of money is shaped by emerging technologies, shifting economic landscapes, and evolving monetary systems. This chapter explores potential developments in the financial world, including digital currencies, blockchain technology, and the changing roles of central banks and financial institutions.

Emerging Technologies in Finance

Digital Currencies and Central Bank Digital Currencies (CBDCs)

- Central Bank Digital Currencies (CBDCs): Many central banks are exploring or piloting digital versions of their national currencies. CBDCs could provide a secure, efficient, and inclusive form of money.

- Benefits: Enhanced financial inclusion, reduced transaction costs, and improved efficiency of monetary policy.

- Challenges: Privacy concerns, cybersecurity risks, and the potential impact on traditional banking systems.

Blockchain and Distributed Ledger Technology (DLT)

- Blockchain Technology: The underlying technology of cryptocurrencies, blockchain provides a decentralized and secure way to record transactions.

- Applications: Beyond cryptocurrencies, blockchain can revolutionize areas such as supply chain management, identity verification, and smart contracts.

- Challenges: Scalability, regulatory hurdles, and energy consumption concerns.

Cryptocurrencies and Decentralized Finance (DeFi)

- Cryptocurrencies: Digital assets like Bitcoin and Ethereum offer alternative forms of money and investment opportunities.

- Potential: Greater financial autonomy, borderless transactions, and the democratization of financial services.

- Risks: High volatility, regulatory uncertainty, and potential for illicit activities.

- Decentralized Finance (DeFi): An ecosystem of financial applications built on blockchain networks that operate without intermediaries.

- Advantages: Increased accessibility, transparency, and reduced costs.

- Risks: Smart contract vulnerabilities, lack of consumer protection, and regulatory challenges.

Shifts in Global Financial Landscapes

Changing Roles of Central Banks

- Enhanced Monetary Policy Tools: Central banks may adopt new tools and strategies to manage digital currencies and integrate them into existing monetary frameworks.

- Financial Stability: Central banks will need to address risks associated with digital currencies and ensure the stability of the financial system.

- Regulatory Oversight: Increased focus on regulating digital financial services and protecting consumers in a rapidly evolving landscape.

Globalization and Financial Integration

- Cross-Border Payments: Advances in digital currencies and blockchain technology could streamline cross-border transactions, reducing costs and increasing efficiency.

- Financial Inclusion: Digital financial services have the potential to reach underserved populations, promoting global economic growth and reducing inequality.

- Regulatory Coordination: As financial markets become more interconnected, international regulatory cooperation will be crucial to manage systemic risks and ensure stability.

Evolution of Monetary Systems

Digital Payment Systems

- Contactless Payments: The rise of contactless payment methods, including mobile wallets and NFC-enabled devices, is changing how consumers transact.

- Convenience: Faster, easier, and more secure transactions.

- Trends: Increased adoption of digital wallets, biometric authentication, and integration with social media platforms.

- Peer-to-Peer (P2P) Payments: Platforms like Venmo, PayPal, and Zelle enable seamless P2P transactions, facilitating the transfer of funds between individuals.

- Growth: Expanding user base and increasing transaction volumes.

- Implications: Disruption of traditional banking services and the need for enhanced cybersecurity measures.

Future Financial Ecosystems

- Open Banking: Regulatory initiatives like the EU's PSD2 and the UK's Open Banking Standard are promoting greater competition and innovation in financial services by allowing third-party access to bank data.

- Benefits: Improved customer experiences, personalized financial products, and increased competition.

- Challenges: Data privacy, security concerns, and the need for robust regulatory frameworks.

- Artificial Intelligence (AI) and Big Data: AI and big data analytics are transforming financial services by enabling more accurate risk assessments, personalized financial advice, and enhanced fraud detection.

- Applications: Robo-advisors, credit scoring, and automated trading.

- Considerations: Ethical concerns, data privacy, and the potential for job displacement.

Speculative Scenarios for the Future of Money

Scenario 1: Digital Currency Dominance

In this scenario, digital currencies, including CBDCs and cryptocurrencies, become the primary forms of money, replacing traditional fiat currencies.

- Impacts: Enhanced financial inclusion, greater economic efficiency, and reduced reliance on traditional banking systems.

- Challenges: Navigating regulatory frameworks, ensuring cybersecurity, and addressing privacy concerns.

Scenario 2: Hybrid Monetary Systems

A hybrid monetary system emerges, where digital currencies coexist with traditional fiat currencies, offering a balance between innovation and stability.

- Impacts: Continued innovation in financial services, greater consumer choice, and improved financial stability.

- Challenges: Coordinating regulatory approaches, managing systemic risks, and ensuring interoperability between different forms of money.

Scenario 3: Centralized Digital Economy

Governments and central banks take a leading role in issuing and regulating digital currencies, creating a highly controlled and centralized digital economy.

- Impacts: Enhanced monetary policy effectiveness, greater financial oversight, and increased control over economic activity.

- Challenges: Potential for reduced financial privacy, increased government surveillance, and the risk of stifling innovation.

Conclusion

The future of money is poised to be shaped by technological advancements, evolving financial landscapes, and changing roles of central banks and financial institutions. Digital currencies, blockchain technology, and AI-driven financial services will play pivotal roles in this transformation. As we navigate these changes, it is crucial to balance innovation with regulatory oversight, ensuring that the benefits of new technologies are realized while managing potential risks. Understanding these dynamics will be essential for policymakers, financial institutions, and consumers as we move towards a more digital and interconnected financial future.